W9-CLP-610

*STRANGE ADVENTURES OF THE GREAT LAKES*

*Also by Dwight Boyer*

TRUE TALES OF THE GREAT LAKES

GHOST SHIPS OF THE GREAT LAKES

GREAT STORIES OF THE GREAT LAKES

# STRANGE
# ADVENTURES
# OF THE
# GREAT LAKES

## by Dwight Boyer

*ILLUSTRATED WITH PHOTOGRAPHS AND MAPS*

FRESHWATER PRESS, INC.

CLEVELAND, OHIO

To a fine son, Larry, and his lovely wife, Lori, and two delightful grandchildren, Dwight II and Ginny Lu, this book is affectionately dedicated.

Copyright © 1974 by Dwight Boyer
All Rights Reserved

No part of this book may be reproduced in any form without the express written permission of Freshwater Press, Inc.

Published & Distributed by
FRESHWATER PRESS, INC.
Cleveland, Ohio

ISBN: 0-912514-52-3
Library of Congress Catalog Card Number: 74-7771

Manufactured in the United States of America

# Contents

# Acknowledgments

Many people with a sincere and personal dedication to our Great Lakes, and fortunately their numbers were legion, had a part in making this book a reality. Some were historians in their own right, with personal collections of note. Others could best be helpful by relating their own experiences. Put together, the hard facts and treasured reminiscences yielded a wide spectrum of color and a unique insight into the lives and times of those who have sailed the lakes in good times and bad.

There could be no more helpful individual to freshwater authors than Janet Coe Sanborn, editor of *Inland Seas,* the quarterly of the Great Lakes Historical Society. Her many kindnesses and professional qualifications shortened many a long road. Fortunately too, many distinguished researchers and authors eased the burdens by their scholarly contributions to *Inland Seas,* among them Rev. Edward J. Dowling, S.J.; Professor Julius F. Wolff, Jr.; Lawrence A. Pomeroy, Jr.; Fred R. Trelfa; and the late C. E. Stein.

Personally tracking down or providing vital and needed

information were Roy Meyer; Georgia S. Cann; Cletus
Schneider; Robert J. MacDonald; Janice H. Gerred; E. J.
"Shine" Sundstrom; Lester H. Bishop; Donna McLeod Rode-
baugh; Duff Brace; Rev. Alexander Meakin; Captain John
Mitchell; James Marshall; Captain George Hanson; Walter
Secord; Captain Ness Matthews; Dan Kissel; Captain John
P. Perkins; John A. Chisholm; Walter and Teddy Remick;
Captain H. C. Inches; James A. Collins; John McHale; Gor-
don Hagadone; Paul Ranahan; Louis LaDuca; Oliver Pohto;
John Zyp; Fred Foote; Randall D. Walthius; Alfred E.
Spragge; Albert J. Zimmer; George Manthey; Harry White-
ley; Carl Ernst; Robert Dyment; and Robert O. Fletcher.

Nor can one discount the value of very personal recollec-
tions of Mrs. John I. Cummings; Captain John Leonard;
Tom Sords; Captain Frank Becker; Durward S. Farr; Cap-
tain James Cowan; Harry Myers; William "Bill" Kennedy;
Captain Joe Fitch; H. R. Whitaker; John Schmitt; Captain
Norbert Fahey; Captain John McCarthy; George Henesey;
George Kitinoja; Arthur O'Connell; Andrew Weisen;
George M. Steinbrenner III; Steve Blossom; Charles U. S.
Grant; William Lockhart; Ben Kimball; Oliver Burnham;
Russ Plumb; Paul S. Peterson, Henry Steinbrenner; Henry
Gerow; and Chuck Zehnder.

Dedicated librarians too sought out seemingly lost details.
Among them were Grace Parch of the *Plain Dealer* library;
Gayle D. Harmer of the St. Clair County (Michigan) Library;
Jean Deyo of the Sarnia (Ontario) Public Library; and Mrs.
Clyde E. Helfter, Curator of Iconography, and Richard M.
Hurst, Chief of Resources, the Buffalo and Erie County His-
torical Society.

Special thanks also go to Milton J. Brown for photographic

contributions; Chester A. Reddeman; Earl C. Hartson; Robert E. Lee; Captain Al Shimin; Rear Admiral Charles A. Curtze, U.S.N. (Ret.); the late Herbert Reynolds Spencer; Vincent Matteucci and Nick Dankovich, *Plain Dealer* artists; and to my wife, Virginia.

A host of Canadian friends also played important roles in gathering material and tracking down facts and people. They include Peggy Gamble Scruton; Verna Gamble; Everett Matthews; Ian M. Macaulay; Captain Wilf Lemcke; Frank Prothero; Bob Scott; Toivo F. Seppala; Maria Hague; Fred Broennle; Ed Flatt; Joseph King; Oscar Anderson; the late Beryl H. Scott; and W. A. W. Catinus, of the Department of Transport.

Most helpful too were the collections of the Fairport Harbor Historical Society and the Western Reserve Historical Society; *Telescope,* the splendid publication of the Great Lakes Maritime Institute; and *The Detroit Marine Historian,* a labor-of-love production of the Marine Historical Society of Detroit.

# 1

## "*Auf Wiedersehen, Lieber Kapitan . . .*
### *Auf Wiedersehen!*"

CAPTAIN NELSON BROWN of the steamer *James H. Reed* was not a man to jump to quick conclusions, and at ten o'clock on the morning of July 12, 1915, what he saw floating on Lake Huron, five miles off Presque Isle, convinced him that he had chanced upon the scene of a recent disaster of major proportions. First of all, on a calm and glassy sea, the *Reed* encountered a considerable field of wreckage . . . numerous timber strongbacks, hatch covers, shreds of tarpaulins, oak cabin doors, mattresses, sections of bunks, odds and ends of furniture and, highly significant in the captain's opinion, more than a dozen floating oil barrels. Captain Brown ordered his vessel stopped for further investigation on the off chance that survivors of what certainly was a shipwreck might still be in the vicinity. By now every member of the *Reed*'s crew were clustered at the rails, some of them poking at the debris with pike poles.

Ordering slow ahead on the engine, the captain circled the area and at last found what seemed to bear out his dire pre-

*1*

dictions. It was a ship's pilot house, apparently blown off by sudden compression of air as the vessel took a quick plunge. Moving nearer, he and the crew could read the ill-fated craft's name board. It was the *Choctaw,* a vessel busily employed in the iron ore and coal trade, owned and managed by the Cleveland-Cliffs Iron Company, of Cleveland. It had been foggy during the night, especially so during the hours just before dawn. But the morning sun was rapidly burning away the fog, and as visibility increased, Captain Brown could see no more wreckage nor any sign of survivors or bodies of unfortunate men who might have perished. To him it was a relatively simple matter of deduction. He well knew the *Choctaw* was a bulk steamer and would not likely be carrying so many barrels of oil unless her engine room department had been blessed with an unusually large supply of lubricating oil. Obviously then, as he duly noted in his log, two vessels, one carrying barrels of oil and probably both steaming at maximum speed, had apparently collided, both going down with all hands. It was a dreadful thing to contemplate, but no other conclusion could be drawn. Hastily noting the clock and almost subconsciously calculating how much time and distance he had sacrificed in probing around the grim scene, he put the *Reed* full ahead and resumed his upbound voyage.

If man occasionally succumbs to a bit of self-satisfaction, it could be forgiven in the instance of Captain Brown on that particular morning. Only the previous afternoon, as the *Reed,* laden with 7600 tons of coal, steamed out of the St. Clair River at Port Huron to meet the gentle swell of Lake Huron, the *Choctaw* had been astern of her. Both vessels encountered fog as soon as they entered the open lake, and it was obvious that it was going to get worse before it got any better. As the situation was one he could do nothing about, Captain Brown established his course for DeTour and the lower St. Marys River, and, almost automatically, as the rules required, checked the *Reed*'s engine down a few revolutions. The half-speed-in-fog rule was almost universally ignored by most shipmasters, even those who recognized the inherent dangers of non-compliance. Their reasoning was purely economic. Slogging along at half speed raised hob with the seasonal tonnage statistics, essentially the sole criteria on which their qualifications were judged in the front office. Unfortunately, those doing the judging were, for the most part, deskbound gentlemen with sharp pencils—white collar, efficiency-minded people whose offices were rarely visited by fog. They knew what it was, recognized it as an occasional inconvenience, but somehow seemed to think that captains should be able to do something about it. When a vessel's tonnage commitments fell in arrears through a skipper's faithful adherence to the prescribed rules, her master was likely to receive a note even sharper than the office pencils.

A cautious, conscientious master, Captain Brown was somewhat critical of Captain Charles Fox of the *Choctaw* when, after both vessels had cleared Port Huron, the *Choctaw*, obviously not checked down in accordance with the rules of navigation and common sense, steamed briskly past the *Reed* and was soon lost in the gray murk. It was even money, too, that the *Choctaw*'s log for that afternoon or the following night would not carry the notation of "fog" but rather "haze," again an almost universal practice to avoid unpleasant complications later should a mishap occur. A vessel in a collision or aground, later determined to be running at full speed when her log indicated fog, could possibly be the last command for her skipper, or at best a suspension of his ticket. Consequently the word "haze" was frequently employed for the distinction between haze and fog, which is a tenuous one and a matter of personal judgment. It was also a term that was difficult to define days later at a hearing before marine authorities and even more obscure months later in a court of law. It was an atmospheric condition that defied concise interpretation or analysis by the shrewdest of admiralty proctors and hence was a favorite term of shipmasters. Captain Brown, peering out at the worsening fog, ruefully concluded that the *Choctaw* would beat him to the Soo Locks by many hours. He trusted that his owners, the Interlake Steamship Company, would be as understanding as they usually were.

The 266-foot *Choctaw* was an unusual vessel in appearance, being a composite of two building styles. Built as one of two sister ships by the Cleveland Ship Building Company in 1892, she featured a rather severe tumblehome, almost as drastic as the whaleback design, but had an almost conventional bow and a wedge-shaped fo'c'sle housing her anchor windlass and dunnage room. She was a straight-deck, seven-hatch boat with no pleasing sheer and with all accommodations aft. She was built to carry about 3000 tons of cargo—coal, iron ore, pig iron or what-have-you—economically and efficiently with the aesthetics of ship design being secondary to practicality.

Launched a couple of days later than her sister ship, the *Andaste*,[1] the *Choctaw* proved to be just what her original owners, the Lake Superior Iron Company, had expected—a sturdy, no-nonsense vessel that carried her burdens comfortably and behaved moderately well in a seaway, although somewhat inclined to wet her deck. But though they were supposed to be sister ships and apparently were in every other respect, sharp-eyed ship buffs soon detected a difference that would escape all but the most observing. Both vessels were seemingly identical when viewed bow-on, like two peas in a pod. The purists, however, gleefully pointed out that the *Andaste* had only three windows across the front of her pilot house, while the *Choctaw* had four! But it was a matter of little moment to the owners, who were concerned only with performance. So out they went into the hard, cruel world of the highly competitive steamboat business with really not anybody caring a whit whether either one had three, four or ten windows.

Among the known hazards of steaming full ahead in a fog on Lake Huron was the distinct possibility of meeting a downbound vessel, probably a Canadian, stem-on, and the likelihood that both would suffer overwhelming damage and founder. It was a ridiculous situation that had persisted since the beginning of lake shipping, although a solution, or partial solution, had always been possible. Alarmed at heavy damage and vessel losses as a result of preventable collisions, the Lake Carriers' Association, an organization of United States lake-vessel owners and managers, had earlier established pre-scribed upbound and downbound courses designed to sepa-rate upbound and downbound navigation by several miles, the upbound course holding nearest to land, the downbound course several more miles offshore. It was an obvious improve-ment over the previous practice of steaming willy-nilly up and down the lake with the possibility of collision increased markedly at night or in hazy or foggy weather. But the Canadian vessel owners, for whatever reasons, had steadfastly refused to cooperate.

The dangers were even more apparent in upper Lake Huron, where upbound and downbound vessels converged near DeTour, and where eastbound and westbound traffic in and out of the Straits of Mackinac was also encountered with great frequency. On a foggy night shoreside residents were treated to a veritable symphony of hoarse steamboat whistles and knew that somewhere out there worried skippers were fretting on their weather bridges, trying to deduce the whereabouts of other vessels and attempting to get bearings on those they judged to be nearest. These were situations that aged captains prematurely and they arose with painful regularity.

Mental visions of many such past occasions were possibly of some consolation for Captain Brown of the *Reed;* at his reduced speed, he should arrive at the congested waters off DeTour late the next day, after a warm August sun had burned off and dissipated the fog. Still, the idea of the *Choctaw* romping blithely ahead rankled. The *Reed* had almost twice the horsepower of the *Choctaw* and was almost twice her size. But she was also carrying more than double the *Choctaw*'s coal cargo and with her engine checked down was destined to fall steadily behind. Both vessels figured prominently in the tonnage and profit factors in their respective fleets and each had been relatively free of groundings or strandings, although the *Choctaw*, when only four years old, had sunk in shallow water near the Soo after colliding with the *L. C. Waldo*. However, she had been raised, promptly repaired and went about her duties as usual.

Another harried shipmaster pertinent to our tale of that

foggy night of August 11 and morning of August 12 was Captain Cornelius Dineen, master of the downbound Canadian steamer *Wahcondah,* Fort William to Montreal with grain. The persistent fog had made the trip down the lower St. Marys River harrowing, and Captain Dineen had enjoyed little or no rest. The 230-foot *Wahcondah,* checked down for the river passage, had behaved perfectly and answered her helm well, but the river is noted for its winding course. Meeting a steady parade of upbound vessels made for a busy and nerve-wrenching night for her master. Nor did the passing of DeTour and the broad and widening waters of upper Lake Huron ease the burdens of command. There was still a steady parade of upbound vessels, and now there was the traffic in and out of the Straits of Mackinac with which to contend. With his whistle blaring out the regulation three blasts at one-minute intervals, Captain Dineen continued on his course without relaxing his alert attention, constantly trying to determine the positions and courses of vessels he could hear but not see.

Strangely, though, or perhaps not so strangely, considering the pressures of the job and the demands of owners, the *Wahcondah's* telegraph, despite the fog, now registered full ahead, eighty-two revolutions per minute which gave her an over-the-water speed of ten and one-half miles per hour. Down in the engine room, second engineer Thomas Hurl would have marked up any subsequent changes on the blackboard for later copying into the scrap log, but none came. The fog, if anything, was even more impenetrable than before, but still the *Wahcondah* drove on as though her master thought she could miraculously make up for lost time merely by being hidden in the anonymity given her by the gray, wet, smothering blanket of fog that lay over all of Lake Huron.

After long, weary hours without sleep Captain Dineen went to his room to rest at 2:10 A.M., soon after the *Wahcondah* passed DeTour. Trying to rest was a travesty under the prevailing conditions. The captain had left orders with first mate David Chambers to call him should upbound steamers be encountered, or if he heard any whistles that might be interpreted as such. Three times between 2:30 and 4:30 A.M. mate Chambers sent the watchman to pound on the captain's door. Three times the exhausted skipper climbed the ladder to the pilot house to assume command in a passing situation. Mate Chambers was apparently an able man, but Captain Dineen could not forget that the twenty-nine-year-old mate had once had masters papers of his own, and that he was now sailing as mate because he had been in a serious accident while commanding the *J. H. Plummer,* putting her ashore under circumstances painfully similar to those that now prevailed. Captain Dineen was taking no chances that lightning might strike twice in the same place.

Somewhere south of the *Wahcondah* the *Choctaw* was still steaming toward DeTour and holding to the inside course advocated by the Lake Carriers' Association. Sometime after midnight, as the fog grew steadily worse and the ominous bellows of steamboat whistles became more frequent, Captain Fox had apparently undergone a change of mind, checking his vessel down to half speed as her own big steam whistle sobbed out an answer to those distant brays.

The twenty-member crew of the *Choctaw* was probably very typical of lake vessels of the era. The deck officers under Captain Fox and the engineers laboring for chief engineer Sherley Shipman were ambitious, career-minded men, but

those in the lower echelons included a variety of nationalities, some recently arrived at our shores, drawn by necessity
to the hard-work, low-pay plight of firemen and coal passers
in the dark hold gang. Such was the lot of Karl Streicher and
Hans Mueller, both firemen. They had left Germany only
months before World War I had ignited the Continent and
welcomed a start in their chosen land however humble their
tasks. They were making satisfactory progress in learning
their new language, Mueller particularly, and indeed, in the
closely knit community aboard ship and in company with
others of various national origins, they probably fared better
afloat than ashore. For despite our protestations of tolerance
and brotherhood, those of German extraction were being
subjected to many jibes, indignities, and even violence. These
were not times of which America could be proud. The British propaganda people did their work well, and the daily
press was consequently laced with their inflamatory and per-
verted fabrications. The rampaging Huns were accused of
raping nuns, bayoneting children, and deliberately shelling
hospitals and orphanages. It was the worst kind of bunkum,
but it had the desired effect of inspiring unreasonable hatred
for Germans and anything German. Anti-German feelings
were running high in the United States, but were even more
evident in Canada, which had quickly joined England in
declaring war after German troops invaded Belgium. The
Dominion had been at war for nearly a year. Union Jacks
flew from every home, store, and factory along the Detroit and
St. Clair rivers. The *Choctaw* was technically in Canadian
waters, a scant couple of hundred feet from shore, when upbound. These were uncomfortable times for men of Teutonic
birth to be working on United States lake vessels. Both Karl

Streicher and Hans Mueller were aware of their rather unusual status. Nor was life made easier by their shipmates,
who achieved a measure of sadistic delight by describing in
exaggerated and horrifying detail their probable fate should
they have the misfortune to tumble overboard in Canadian
waters.

It was 5:00 A.M. when Captain Dineen returned to his
room after the third interruption since the *Wahcondah*
passed DeTour at 2:00 A.M., but he had been resting only
about ten minutes when again came the pounding on his
door by the watchman.

"Steamer whistle, sir."

Bounding up the ladder once more he was met by mate
Chambers, who stated that he could hear a fog whistle from
another boat, that it was relatively close, and that the steamer
in question must have just started sounding signals, otherwise he would have heard it and summoned the skipper
sooner.

Captain Dineen grabbed the whistle lever and blew three
quick blasts, shortly answered by the other vessel, upon which
the captain sounded the *Wahcondah*'s whistle twice. This was
answered, as was a second two-whistle signal by the captain,
the sound appearing to be about two points off the *Wahcondah*'s starboard side. The whistle blasts, difficult to judge in
the fog, would indicate that the other vessel was passing directly across the *Wahcondah*'s course. Captain Dineen took
the helm and swung the wheel frantically, turning his vessel
hard starboard to clear whatever boat was out there in the
opaque gray mist. Visibility was about seventy feet beyond
the steamer's steering pole. More whistle signals were exchanged, but it was too late. Directly across the *Wahcondah*'s

bow there slid the long black shape that was the *Choctaw!* Captain Dineen was still clutching the steering-wheel spokes when his vessel cut into the *Choctaw* between her number one and two hatches, and indeed, had not the impact point been at the junction of heavy framing, the *Wahcondah* might have halved her on the spot. As it was, her stem cut into the *Choctaw* about eight feet, a mortal wound in any event. The *Wahcondah*'s bow was crushed in from the bulwarks to her forefoot, and the *Choctaw*'s forward motion twisted her stem to port.

The instant he saw a collision was inevitable, Captain Dineen automatically threw the telegraph lever to full astern. Down below engineer, Thomas Hurl had immediately responded by reversing the engine. The *Choctaw*'s forward speed and the *Wahcondah*'s engine working full astern soon pulled the two vessels apart. The *Choctaw* drifted out of sight in the fog as Captain Dineen ordered his lifeboats swung out and rushed down below to check his own damage. He found the forepeak filling with water and quickly put some of the crew to stuffing the ruptured plates with mattresses, pillows and blankets. Then, convinced that his own vessel would not sink, at least for a considerable time, he returned to the pilot house to steer clumsily in the direction in which the *Choctaw* had disappeared. Mate Chambers and watchman Charles Cleson affirmed that they could hear shouts from the other vessel, whose name had as yet not been ascertained . . . voices calling out that they were sinking. Shortly the *Choctaw* came into view, badly down by the head, her crew launching her lifeboats. Convinced that his own boats would not be needed, Captain Dineen steamed the sluggish *Wahcondah* in to pick up the survivors.

Captain Fox, standing in the second and last boat to leave his stricken steamer, stood up as if in respect for an old friend as the crew watched in awe. She went down, when she had made up her mind, first listing to port, then rolling to starboard for a time before her stern rose out of the water. Then she rolled over completely and went down, bottom side up amid thunderous noises as cold water hit her hot boilers and bulkheads blew out, spewing out the contents of her cabins and quarters.

"It sounded as if millions of dishes and hundreds of sticks were being broken," Captain Fox later told a friend.

At this point he remembered that, although he and chief engineer Shipman had managed to save most of the *Choctaw*'s important papers, he had forgotten $160 in the safe. Second mate Hans Larson had rushed up to the deck at the instant of the collision but had quickly returned to his room to retrieve a new suit. But the vessel was filling so rapidly that he abandoned the attempt and barely escaped with his life.

Slowly the *Wahcondah,* steering rather erratically because of her twisted stem, pulled close to the *Choctaw*'s boats and took aboard the crew. The empty lifeboats, the only surviving wreckage of any value, were hoisted on deck by sheer manpower.

There was no point in a discussion of each other's navigational shortcomings, so both Captains Fox and Dineen avoided the subject, knowing full well that hasty statements, however innocuous they seemed at the time, must surely surface in the hearings and litigation that would inevitably follow. Captain Dineen knew that the wreck commissioner's court, in Kingston, would be particularly sticky since the *Wahcondah*'s wheat cargo was destined for Montreal and transshipment to England, where shortages were already serious due to the German submarine successes. Luckily, his own damage had been largely confined to the stem and forepeak area. He doubted that more than a couple of hundred bushels of grain had been wetted. It is interesting to note that it was three to four hours after the collision before first mate Chambers got around to entering in the *Wahcondah*'s log the details of whistle signals and events leading up to the *Choctaw*'s sinking.

The *Choctaw*'s crew was made as comfortable as possible, and by that unique unanimity of thinking that so often follows tragic events, the subject of the collision was avoided as a topic of conversation. The *Wahcondah* steamed on, still steering erratically despite the ballast chief engineer William McLaren pumped into her aft tanks to bring her bow and twisted stem up higher. She limped along at four miles per hour, a pace that, had it been maintained in the fog after passing DeTour, would probably have prevented the collision.

Sitting on a hatch with mugs of tea in hand, Karl Streicher and Hans Mueller were maintaining a discreet silence, smiling and nodding when spoken to by the *Wahcondah*'s crewmen, knowing full well that their accents would immediately pinpoint their Teutonic origins. Their worst fears had been confirmed when, at daybreak, they saw the watchman putting up the Union Jack, and black despair was in their hearts after they heard crew members say that the vessel would probably put in at Sarnia, Ontario, for examination by the underwriters before proceeding to Windsor, the nearest yard with repair facilities.

For Karl Streicher and Hans Mueller the war had suddenly become very real and very near. Now they were sure, through no fault of their own, they were about to be delivered into the hands of one of the Fatherland's bitterest enemies, a Canada so thoroughly aroused that they could only guess what their fate might be. Visions of jail and of being paraded through the streets like hunted animals flitted before them.

"*Mein Gott,*" moaned Karl Streicher, "*besser tot als das.*"

"*Ja,*" agreed Hans Mueller. "Better death than that."

The *Wahcondah* was far away and hull down on the horizon when the heavily laden *James H. Reed* chanced on the wreck scene. The warm morning sun had made short work of the fog, but the sea was littered with sundry evidence that at least one of the vessels in collision had foundered so quickly that the air pressure built up by a catastrophic inrush of water had burst off her accommodations, gutting her like a codfish. The many oil barrels were a positive indication in Captain Brown's opinion that the second vessel had been carrying a partial deck load of oil. The barrels, as a matter of fact, had been lashed to the *Choctaw*'s boat deck and were to have been unloaded at the Soo for transfer to other Cleveland-Cliffs vessels.

Yes, the *Choctaw*, which had so blithely steamed ahead of the *Reed* only the previous afternoon, had now been consigned to the deep. Captain Brown, very familiar with his charts, knew that she had gone down in about 250 feet of water. He grimly noted his observations in the *Reed*'s log and clucked his tongue over the sad fate of her crew.

The *Reed* had no wireless, and Captain Brown could not report his findings until his vessel reached the Soo locks. There the news caused a flurry of excitement and much spec-

ulation as to the identity of the other steamer. The word was
quickly flashed over the wires, and the next morning's edi-
tion of the *Cleveland Plain Dealer* carried a banner headline
about Captain Brown's sensational discovery far up Lake
Huron, off Alpena, Michigan. "Forty Probably Lost in Lake
Collision," said the newspaper, citing the theory expressed
by the captain that two vessels had crashed together in the
fog and both had gone down.

It was distressing news the Cleveland-Cliffs people were
obliged to send to the next of kin of the apparently lost sailors, terse telegrams that said so little but still so much,
creating aching hearts in distant homes. Some of those missing were from Cleveland and for them the news was carried
by personnel of the company's marine department. One of
the recipients was the wife of chief engineer Sherley Shipman
and a bride of only seven months. When the news came she
was reading a letter from her husband that had arrived only
that morning. Similar tidings were borne to two other Cleveland homes, those of first mate Lars Bru and assistant engineer John J. Higgins.

Meanwhile, with Captain Fox nervously pacing the deck
and mentally composing the telegram he would send to the
*Choctaw*'s owners, the *Wahcondah* approached the dock at
Sarnia. Workmen on the premises quickly noted her bashed-
in bow, and their excited shouts and gestures brought others
running from the freight sheds and provision houses.

The commotion was not lost on the unhappy pair of Germans, but was unfortunately misinterpreted. Seconds earlier
they had cast envious glances across the St. Clair river where,
only a scant few hundred feet away, lay Port Huron and
freedom. But the current at that point, near where the water

of Lake Huron pours in, was like a millrace and survival for a swimmer would be highly unlikely.

*"Das meint einsperrung fuer uns,"* groaned Karl Streicher in a sepulchral groan.

*"Ja,"* sighed Mueller. "It's internment for us."

Captain Dineen gave word for the lines to be thrown, but his mind was very probably on a telegram he must send, too, for he knew that it would generate a series of depositions, innumerable embarrassing questions and inevitably an official Dominion hearing by the Wreck Commission's Court. The next few days would be busy ones.

Captain Dineen had reversed the *Wahcondah's* engine to take the way off his vessel, and Captain Fox was still nervously pacing the deck when he was distracted by unusual activity at the fantail. First there was a sharp report, a gaggle of green boards flying upwards and then, horror of horrors, he spotted Karl Streicher and Hans Mueller sheepishly coiling up what seemed to be a small boat painter.

"What the hell is going on?" he demanded.

The crestfallen pair could only stand there, shoulders sagging, peering furtively over in the direction of Port Huron and the United States flag that flew so briskly near the life-saving station.

*"Mein Gott, was wird mit uns geschehen?"* sobbed Streicher.

*"Ja, mein Gott,* what will become of us?" lamented Mueller.

Captain Dineen and various members of both crews were also drawn to the scene of highly unusual shenanigans on the fantail of the *Wahcondah,* glimpsing what appeared to be pieces of the vessel's green yawl boat being thrown hither and yon. Captains Fox and Dineen, hands on hips and looking exceedingly grim, stood in the center of what seemed to the forlorn Germans a menacing group.

"All right, let's have it," gritted Captain Fox.

"Yes, yes, what's this all about?" said the impatient Captain Dineen.

"Ah, *danke schoen, dear Kapitans,*" faltered Hans Mueller. "I thank you for hearing us out. Ve are, as you say, in a problem."

Then, haltingly, but with all the sincerity that comes to men seemingly on the brink of the gallows, Karl Streicher and Hans Mueller poured out their story. They were, both admitted, so sure in their own minds that they would be clapped into prison by the Canadians, and perhaps be interned for years, that they had sought to escape their hopeless predicament by rowing across the river to United States soil in the *Wahcondah's* little yawl boat. But the long painter and the adverse and conflicting currents when Captain Dineen had reversed the vessel's engine had swung the yawl under the stern and into the propeller before they could draw it alongside. They were not murderous Huns, they asserted, merely honest seamen trying to make a new life for themselves, with an abiding fear and horror of being incarcerated for years for still being, technically, citizens of an enemy country.

"*Besser tot als das,*" entreated Karl Streicher.

"*Ja,*" avowed Hans Mueller, "better death than that."

Despite their own very serious problems both captains could readily see the humor in the situation and sympathized with the unfortunate pair, now literally shaking in their boots and still casting envious eyes across the river at Port

Huron and freedom. Resisting a strong inclination to smile, Captain Fox motioned them to stay where they were and drew Captain Dineen aside to explain that both were good men who had already applied for their first citizenship papers. Captain Dineen agreed that he and Fox had too much on their minds at the moment to become involved in what could possibly develop into an international incident. Besides, no useful purpose would be accomplished in detaining the two terrified firemen.

The Dutchmen's dilemma, however, was already being resolved. Unbeknownst to them, Captain Fox had agreed that his crew might lower one of the salvaged lifeboats and row across to Port Huron. The Sarnia dock foreman had advised him that wire stories from the Soo had already reported the apparent sinking of the *Choctaw* with all hands. The crew, he knew, would be frantic in their anxiety to notify their families by phone or wire that they were indeed still alive and drawing paychecks. He, Captain Fox, would stay in Sarnia long enough to call his owners and report the facts, a rather unpleasant task that also awaited Captain Dineen. Both knew that this was only the beginning of a long series of official investigations, depositions and litigation that might drag on for a couple of years.

When the *Choctaw*'s port lifeboat had been drawn alongside and was becoming crowded with her crew, Captain Dineen beckoned to the unhappy Germans. "Off you go," he ordered, "and let's hear no more of this internment business."

With the weight of the world no longer on their shoulders, the delighted firemen bounded into the boat with hoarse cries of deliverance and many appreciative *danke shoens* to Captain Dineen.

But it was a worried and pensive crew that drew briskly against the fierce current that boils down the St. Clair River from Lake Huron, knowing surely that their loved ones at this very moment considered them dead and gone. Each in his own mind was picturing the scenes of sorrow at home. And for chief engineer Sherley Shipman there was that bride of seven months who would be overjoyed to hear that, as in the case of Mark Twain, his death had been grossly exaggerated.

None of these family considerations were issues of importance to the two overjoyed firemen, late of Germany. Standing in the lifeboat as their companions labored against the current, their eyes and hearts were dedicated to a man who stood pensively on the *Wahcondah*'s spar deck. He wore the four stripes of a captain and what could have been a trace of a smile on his face.

*"Ach, mein Kapitan,"* shouted Karl Streicher, *"Danke schoen, danke schoen und auf wiedersehen."*

*"Ja,"* roared Hans Mueller. *"Danke shoen, lieber Kapitan and auf wiedersehen . . . auf wiedersehen!"*

---

[1] The *Andaste* lasted fourteen years longer than her sister ship, the *Choctaw*, vanishing with all hands on Lake Michigan on a wild night in September, 1929.

# 2

*Please Pass the Pancakes*

For a man who was to become a legend in his own time, "Jumbo" Lynch departed this sorry world with two rather elementary mysteries unsolved, or at least unrecalled, by scores of men who sailed with him. One was his first name which, depending upon who is trying to do the recalling, was Al, which might mean Alfred, Albert or Aloysius. According to others, it could be Henry, Herman, James, Vincent or Patrick. It is doubtful that the question was ever put to him aboard ship or at least it was never pressed, for Jumbo was often, nay, usually, of truculent mien, disinclined to bandy the usual amenities with any but a few chosen friends. Captain Norbert Fahey, who earned the nickname of "K.O." for his pugilistic bent as a young wheelsman, thinks it was Al, but is distrustful of his memory, too. The second mystery was the town or city of his origin, again variously recalled as Buffalo, Manistee, Anchor Bay, Pensaukee or Algonac. Merrill Kingsbury, who began his career with Jumbo on the old *W. D. Rees* in 1919 and rose to be vice-president of Wilson

"JUMBO" LYNCH

Marine Transit Company, thinks he came from Anchorville, Michigan, but, like Captain Fahey, isn't quite sure. But again, transient shipmates, noting his size and aware of his incendiary temperament, were not inclined to be persistent about either his name or birthplace, philosophically attributing his abrasive disposition to the fact that he was usually hungry, which, ironically, was why he was so frequently unemployed. For the nickname of Jumbo, which inspires a vision of a gentle buffoon of notable girth, was, in his case, not a tribute to his disposition or physical dimensions, which were considerable, but to his appetite which was even more considerable.

The latter fact in itself, after one becomes cognizant of Jumbo's qualifications at the mess table, seems to pose still another mystery: how he lived so long without being violently done in by one of the many long-suffering shipboard practitioners of the culinary arts. Certainly he gave them just and sufficient cause.

Unschooled, somewhat grotesque and always the unlovable oaf, Jumbo was, to the cooks, their gall and wormwood, their crown of thorns, their trial by fire, their cross to bear, a budget-wrecking, moonfaced Gargantua of the galley whose insatiable appetite drove many of them to partake frequently of lemon extract and, when ashore, of even more ardent spirits.

An itinerate fireman in the days of hand-fired boilers, Jumbo wielded a No. 4 coal scoop with some proficiency, exhibited a like skill and dedication in drinking habits, but achieved his ultimate triumph at the crew's mess table where he devoured food in such quantities as to bring tears of rage and frustration to the eyes of those who labored over the old galley coal ranges. A typical breakfast might include twenty or thirty pancakes, a dozen eggs, endless rashers of bacon and enough toast to stuff a seabag, all washed down with a gallon of coffee. Lunches and dinners were even more heroic in proportion.

Any captain likes to have a happy ship which, in many cases, is achieved by being assigned, year after year, a cook of unquestioned talent and of a cheerful disposition. Then, obviously, by providing him with the makings of hearty, stick-to-the-ribs steamboat food, the salubrious shipboard climate prevails. It was a simple-enough formula until the boat was short of firemen and an unthinking commissioner at the local Lake Carriers' Association assembly room assigned Jumbo to the firehold. Shortly thereafter, or when the fact became known in the galley, cooks were wont to wax eloquent, behave churlishly and bang their pots and pans around in a great show of intemperance. For the very presence of Jumbo, the humble fireman, was likely to precipitate what cooks feared most, a sharp note from the shoreside brass when they saw the supply list, demanding to know what the hell the cook thought he was running, a mess hall on a troop ship? Tempers, consequently, were likely to flare and unhappiness become so general in the galley as to make a mockery of the happy ship of the pre-Jumbo era.

Cooks, like many skippers of the times, preferred keeping their contacts with management at a bare minimum. But then, as is often the case today, they were saddled with shore-dictated formulas of a specific number of cents per meal, per man, a specious bit of budgetary shenanigans which, with the bulk of Jumbo aboard, had no relationship to reality. Jumbo, never known for tact or diplomacy, would snuggle his 365 pounds down on the mess-room bench and proceed to consume more food than the combined total of the other eight or ten gentlemen present. Indeed, when the others had finished, they were likely to congregate out on the deck and peer in awe through the portholes at the spectacle of Jumbo, still eating and cleaning out every dish and bowl provided for the family-style meals. He was the Titan of the table, the colossus of chow, the glutton of the Great Lakes!

As men of the same craft or trade are bound together by mutual pride in their careers, it followed that for cooks the problem of Jumbo had to be met and resolved with some show of firmness. Room for the individuality of the culinary specialist could be expressed in whatever manner seemed appropriate in any given emergency. And emergencies were always in vogue when Jumbo's ponderous bulk loomed over the boarding ladder. They were met with whatever ingenuity and action time permitted, not all of the procedures ethical in the strictest interpretation, but most effective.

The direct-actionists, concluding that unemployment was better than the thankless job of trying to satisfy his appetite or justify skyrocketing grocery orders, simply packed their gear and departed. Others, made of sterner stuff, also packed their gear, but it was merely visual evidence of an ultimatum to the captain! "Either he goes or I do." Unfortunately for Jumbo, few skippers relished having their galley staff decimated, since the cook usually took with him his assistants, who were also aware of the futility of trying to feed the always-ravenous fireman. The same threat of an unmanned galley was also an ugly possibility if the cook happened to be "uptown" when Jumbo was signed on, and learned of his presence later only by the astronomical quantities of eggs, bacon and pancakes being borne into the crew's mess room. The rebellion was inevitable, as was the word to the captain: "If he doesn't get off at the Soo, I do." Again, the prospect of the cooks departing midway in a voyage usually resulted in Jumbo being paid off at the Soo locks.

Another approach to the problem was that practiced with some frequency by "Corned Beef" Jim Lovely, cook on the *John W. Gates* and other vessels of the Pittsburgh Steamship

Company to which he was seasonally assigned. It was simple. It was quick. It was bribery. And it worked.

As recalled by Captain John P. Perkins, Lovely's technique involved but three basic elements. First, advance knowledge from the chief engineer that a fireman was being paid off, indicating an immediate replacement. Secondly, when this information was forthcoming, it necessitated a sharp watch on the dock gate to spot the new man. Thirdly, if by chance the waddling bulk of Jumbo loomed at the watchman's shanty, a frantic pooling of monetary resources by the galley staff. The harvest, entrusted to Lovely, would be waiting for Jumbo at the bottom of the boarding ladder, along with a firm hint that he should take it and get lost. Jumbo, probably with more cash than he would have cleared had he sailed and been paid off at the Soo, would shuffle back to the assembly room, complaining of some sudden indisposition.

Jumbo lived, worked and established his reputation in times now often termed "the good old days," although in truth they were far from good. It was an era of low pay for non-licensed personnel, long hours, hard work and an industrial climate that discouraged stability of employment in the lower echelons of the steamboating business. With none of the security benefits of today, firemen, coal passers, deckhands, oilers and wipers were a restless lot, signing off and on perhaps a dozen or more vessels during a season. For these itinerate traits they were often referred to as "trippers," men who signed on with no intention of making more than a trip or two, just enough to get a little spending or drinking money. While captains and engineers would have been much happier with a stable work force under them, the authority to achieve this enviable status was not divested in them.

First mates, by the nature and requirements of their jobs, were traditionally assigned the responsibility of signing on new help and paying off those leaving, for whatever reason. Like captains and chief engineers they deplored the routine of hiring or paying off trippers. Most of them had a simple yardstick for judging whether a man was coming aboard for only a trip or if he intended to stay, the judgment being rendered on the basis of the personal gear he brought aboard. If he had only a spare shirt or a pair of overalls tucked under an arm, it was unfailingly the uniform of a tripper and unless the need was desperate he would be turned away. If, however, he hauled up a suitcase of some bulk and heft, he could be counted upon for more lasting tenure. But the trippers soon learned of this basic assessment and countered with their own devious subterfuges. The trick was to invest twenty-five cents in a secondhand, cardboard, please-don't-rain suitcase, the kind that usually collapsed when wet. This, loaded with old magazines and sometimes a brick or two wrapped in what little clothing the tripper possessed, would pass the weight test of the mates. Such a man was Jumbo Lynch who, in his heyday, was better known on the lakes than the most honored of skippers or revered tycoons of the shipping industry. He was one of a kind. In waterfront bistros from Duluth to Buffalo, in fo'c'sles, in engine rooms and in the assembly rooms or hiring halls the tales of his prowess at the crew's mess tables abounded. All this in an age when food was the only fringe benefit offered, and gastronomical excesses were the order of the day for others of his ilk and following, men with large appetites and colorful names like "Scrapiron" Kelley, "Lopsided" Jake, "Pickles" O'Brien, "Germany George" Jessup, "Fairport" Riley, "Sandusky" Hank, "Slice Bar" Steve,

"Pittsburgh Blackie," "Milwaukee Dutch" Miller, "Boxcar" Murphy, "Shantytown" Bill Mittleman, Carl "The Terrible Swede" Gust, "Four-Track Red" Hall and a couple of heavy-eating brothers from Ashtabula, Ohio, known only as "Ham and Eggs." But all were mere adolescents at the table compared to Jumbo.

It is safe to say that no man in Great Lakes history sailed on more boats than Jumbo, thanks to his appetite, the itinerate nature of firemen and the industrial atmosphere of his times. Frequently it was the individual characteristic of some fire holds that caused Jumbo and others to shun them except when in pressing need of funds or food and even then making the duration of their stays as brief as possible. It was a known fact that some boats had evil reputations as being "hard firing," or, in other words, had boilers requiring a maximum of physical effort to keep them producing the prescribed steam pressure for the engines. Such vessels were likely to generate frequent openings for firemen and coal passers, boats to be studiously avoided when men of such skills had a choice of jobs. But for Jumbo, his financial condition perilous and his appetite insatiable, there was often no choice.

To those who ruled the galleys and were unfortunate enough to encounter Jumbo in his prime the experiences were memorable, especially when viewed after the passage of time and when the luxury of philosophy can be applied. Such a man is Gordon Hagadone, a shipboard cook for forty-two years, the last twenty-four with the Cleveland-Cliffs fleet. Hagadone was lord and master in the galley of the *Pere Marquette No. 19,* a Lake Michigan carferry, one bitter winter in the early 1920s when Jumbo chanced to join the fire hold gang.

"It was tough sailing in the winter," he recalls, "cold and rough all the way between Ludington and Milwaukee, so rough that one day I had the dinner roll off the stove three times. The company recognized the hardships of winter sailing and placed no limit on the food, although some lines held the cook to eighteen or nineteen cents per meal, per man. One day the mate, Harry Cromberg, sort of challenged me to fill Jumbo up. He said to do it no matter what the cost, and if there was any squawk from the old man that he'd take care of it. Well, sir, I cooked him a whole pork loin and cut it into twenty-four chops. And damned if he didn't eat every one of them, along with a couple of big bowls of vegetables, about a peck of potatoes, mashed, and three whole loaves of my home-baked bread. Even then he sort of looked around, wistfully, as if hoping more would be coming. He had downed as much as six or seven ordinary men."

One of Hagadone's most refreshing memories is an incident he witnessed one day in Milwaukee when Jumbo and a traveling salesman met, a traumatic experience for the salesman, an unexpected bonanza for Jumbo.

"There was this tavern at Mitchell and Kinnickinnic Streets, where the sailors used to hang around between jobs. Jumbo was there, hungry and broke as usual, when this salesman came in to talk to the proprietor. Well, Jumbo sidles up to the salesman and hits him up for some change. The salesman, thinking that he wanted it for a drink, says no, but that if he was hungry he would take him to the nearby restaurant and fill him up. Brother, he didn't know what was coming. We did, and some of us went along to watch. In those days you could buy a chicken dinner, complete with dumplings, vegetables and the works, for thirty-five cents. The poor guy just stood there speechless while Jumbo dug in, but when the bill had reached five dollars he cut him off. The salesman was so impressed that he arranged to meet Jumbo at the same place the next Sunday for a repeat performance, saying that he wanted to bring some friends along to watch, that they wouldn't believe him otherwise."

Later both Jumbo and Hagadone sought the more temperate climes of the lower lakes to ply their respective trades, although never again were their paths to cross.

"He used to like to work on the 'line' boats, the package and passenger boats operated by the railroads," reminisces Paul Ranahan, a wheelsman when he and Jumbo were shipmates on the *Utica* of the Great Lakes Transit Company.

"He was so big that he would completely fill up the door into the fire hold, like a tennis ball in a kitchen drain, but he moved about pretty lively when the porter rang the meal bell. He'd sit down to the breakfast table, and when the porter would bring out a big platter of pancakes, eggs and bacon he'd just pull the whole platter over in front of him and start eating. All the other men would have to wait for more eggs and bacon, but by that time Jumbo would be ready for another helping. The 'line' boats were not on a budget and old 'Roast Beef' Charlie Hone of the *Tionesta* used to do his best to fill him up, but if he ever did Jumbo wouldn't admit it."

Louis LaDuca, who for years operated the Frontier Marine Supply Company, in Buffalo, has lively memories of the donnybrook that nearly ensued the day he delivered the grocery order to the steamer *Herbert F. Black*. "It was nearly supper time and the cook was busy so we left some items out on the deck where it was cool, including a bushel of apples. Jumbo was wandering around and picked up one to eat. It wasn't long until the dinner bell rang, but by that time he had eaten the whole bushel. But he still went in and ate enough for five men."

There were times when his outrageous excesses nearly brought Jumbo to an untimely end, under circumstances that might inspire a judge, after hearing the details, to render a verdict of "justifiable homicide."

Such a long-ago occasion is recalled by Captain Arthur W. Dana, then a fourteen-year-old deckhand on the *Robert L. Fryer* of the old Mitchell fleet. The *Fryer* was about to enter one of the Soo locks, upbound, when Jumbo rose from the breakfast table after demolishing a dozen eggs, thirty-five pancakes, a pound of bacon and a towering stack of toast. He settled himself on a hatch, rocked frequently by blissful rumbles of digestion as he kept a toothpick busy. An acquaintance standing on the lock wall spotted him and called over: "How do you like working on the *Fryer?*"

"O.K.," replied Jumbo, "except that she don't feed so good."

Those around him burst out laughing, but the cook, who also chanced to be within earshot, literally went berserk. He grabbed a fire ax, and would have ended the fireman's career then and there had not strong arms and cooler heads prevailed. Even so, the cook rushed to the pilot house to issue the usual ultimatum, "Either he goes or I do," to Captain Russell Hemenger.

"Don't worry," said Hemenger, soothingly, "he'll be getting off at Duluth. He never makes more than one trip, just enough to get a little money. Then he's off to the jungle until he's broke again."

Jumbo made a lasting impression on Charles U. S. Grant, who, in 1922, was a deckhand aboard the *William R. Linn* of the Pittsburgh Steamship Company. Still in high school in Lakewood, Ohio, Grant and two chums, Irwin Marshall and Bill Lockhart, worked summers on the lake boats.

"Jumbo had been paid off at the Soo by another boat," Grant remembers. "The *Linn* needed a fireman desperately so he was hired. We were also short of coal passers so Captain Bill McLaughlin sent me down to the fire hold to help out. We would usually try to beat Jumbo to the breakfast table, but rarely did. Then, after we had managed to get something to eat, some of us would gather outside the crew's mess and watch Jumbo through the porthole. He practically inhaled pancakes and eggs. The cooks, a black man and his wife, threatened to get off the boat at our destination, Ashland, Wisconsin, simply because with Jumbo aboard they spent all their time in the galley. Jumbo had practically no neck, huge arms and shoulders and in his bib overalls was a rather ludicrous spectacle."

Between brief periods of employment Jumbo and others of his itinerant calling lived in the various "jungles," at nearly every lake port, a hobo-like existence that may well have been an early version of today's communes. Between Gary and South Chicago a railroad trestle gave shelter to the nomads of the deck and fire hold. In Toledo the camp was in the old Ironwood district and similar such encampments were fixtures at Duluth, Buffalo, Milwaukee and even the Soo, although here it was strictly a summertime affair due to the rigorous climate. But perhaps the most exotic of the jungles was at Conneaut, Ohio, then as now a major coal-shipping and iron-ore-receiving port. The oasis was just west of town, on the site of what is now Conneaut Township Park. Here the vagabonds of the lakes built shelters made of old hatch tarpaulins in which to take their ease. A hole drilled in a small gas line they discovered provided the eternal flame for cooking or warmth. They accumulated the pots and pans necessary and daily canvassed the local bakery for day-old items, the butcher shops for scraps of meat, and dunned householders for canned goods. One of the rascals would be delegated to rise early in the morning to follow closely on the heels of the milkman, pilfering the camp's needs from porches. But milk was a minor item. The staff of life for many of the residents was stronger stuff—homemade wine, bootleg booze and often, when funds were low, Sterno or canned heat, a paste-like substance which, when melted, yielded practically pure alcohol. George Kitinoja, who lives almost on the exact site of the old jungle today, doesn't remember Jumbo as much of a drinker.

"Hell, he couldn't afford to drink. It took all his money to eat!"

In his earlier years on the boats Jumbo may indeed have been a gentle, soft-spoken fellow as some vaguely recollect. But according to Kitinoja, he had an erratic, mostly surly disposition, again blamed by friends on the fact that he was usually hungry. In any event, because of his size, petulance and obvious power, few would risk tangling with him, and it was a contentious reputation he seemed to enjoy.

For some reason Jumbo had a fondness for Conneaut where even today wondrous tales of his capacity for food are told by men who knew him. One of them is George Henesey, a sailor himself for forty-one years, rising from porter to first mate.

"Another haunt for sailors was the Seamen's Bethel, at the northeast corner of Day Street and Park Avenue," he happily recalls. "It was operated by the Congregational Church and managed by Adam Tate. It was sort of a temporary haven and provided bunks, a reading room and, of course, evening and Sunday services. Jumbo, by this time, had been blackballed by many shipping lines, although occasionally a skipper, feeling sorry for him, would invite him aboard for a meal, give him a day's wages and send him 'back up the hill.' Between these rare treats he quite often used to sit on the steps of the Bethel and sailors going down to, or coming from, the docks would toss him a quarter or fifty cents. When he had accumulated enough he would go across the street to the Greek restaurant operated by Gus Pappas and get himself something to eat."

"The Bethel was some place," reminisces George Kitinoja. "There were men of many nationalities sailing in those days so on a warm night the front steps would be sort of an early-day United Nations. The joke of the town was that when the Bethel finally burned down the word that flashed around was that six thousand lives were lost—all of them bedbugs."

Both Bill Ford, the Lake Carriers' Association commissioner at Conneaut, and his assistant, Abe Harris, were sympathetic to Jumbo's appetite and got him jobs whenever they could, the opportunities growing fewer as his choleric disposition and appetite grew to legendary proportions. Chief engineers, even though they might be urgently in need of a fireman, would specify that Jumbo wasn't welcome. Nothing personal mind you, but there just wasn't any sense in triggering off a crisis in the galley.

There came a day, inevitably, when Jumbo was taken on as a fireman and forever departed his Conneaut haunts. In all likelihood, since he was still a dedicated tripper and eater, he was paid off at the Soo, Duluth, Milwaukee or Chicago. Then he simply disappeared, gone for many weeks and months from the fire holds and the convenient jungles!

One day in Chicago, along the waterfront, Paul Ranahan, the young wheelsman when Jumbo was working on the *Utica,* spotted what seemed to be an oddly familiar face topping a painfully thin and emaciated-looking body. It was Jumbo!

"He said that he had been in the Marine Hospital, in Chicago," recalls Ranahan, "where they had removed a record-length tapeworm from him."

Strangely, Gordon Hagadone, the former cook on the *Pere Marquette No. 19,* happened to be in the Marine Hospital the next winter and saw the tapeworm.

"As I remember, it was darned near thirty feet long," says Hagadone. "They had it in a jar of alcohol."

Actually, tapeworms (diphyllobothrium) were a real, recognized and relatively common affliction in the days before electric refrigeration. They were parasitic to man, with the larvae usually found in fish. Sometime, long years before, Jumbo had devoured an overly ripe fish. There are instances of specimens measuring twenty to thirty feet in length. Jumbo's, if it was consistent with his physical dimensions, could very well have been a whopper. But the tapeworm credited to Jumbo varies in length from four to thirty feet, depending upon who is doing the recalling and what the years have done to memories. These variances notwithstanding, the tapeworm was very real and was undoubtedly responsible for Jumbo becoming the most talked-about man on the lakes.

It would be gratifying to report that once the appetite mystery was resolved and corrected that Jumbo returned happily to his trade a new man. But the ominous fact is that he just vanished from all his accustomed hangouts, and his associates saw him no more. Although he was still the subject of hundreds of numerous fo'c'sle and pilot-house yarns, the man who inspired them was strangely missing. And now that they paused to recall the incidents so vivid in the past, those who knew him suddenly realized that they could not remember ever hearing his first name. Nor, for another thing, did they know where he was from. He began as a man of mystery and ended as one, perhaps in some potter's field, far from the nostalgic sobs of steamboat whistles, the clang of a No. 4 coal scoop and the welcoming ring of the porter's dinner bell.

In his time Jumbo Lynch enraged, frustrated, elevated the blood pressures and ruined the dispositions of more steamboat cooks than any man in history, and passed on probably without knowing that his ferocious appetite made at least one friend in a galley.

Albert J. Zimmer, long an agent for the Lake Carriers' Association, likes to reminisce about the time he was talking to a cook who had just completed a trip on which Jumbo had been a fireman, witnessing firsthand the seemingly sleight-of-hand disappearance of astonishing quantities of food.

"What would be your reaction if Jumbo decided to sign on for another trip?" asked Zimmer.

"Well," philosophized the cook, "Jumbo has already learned to eat, and while I am not the best cook on the lakes,

I am still learning. So, I suppose that a second trip by him would be a compliment to me."

And poor Jumbo, up in that Valhalla of bountiful harvest tables reserved for heroic eaters, would be profoundly grateful for the news.

# 3

~~~~~~~~~~~~

~~~~~~~~

~~~~

## *The Matriarch of Misery Bay*

A~NY ILLUSIONS~ Americans may have as to the esteem
and honor in which the United States Navy holds its historic
vessels, the *Constitution* [1] notwithstanding, should be completely shattered by an account of what happened to its first
iron vessel. Contrary to the perpetuated myths of schoolbook
history, this was not the *Monitor* of Civil War fame, but the
old U.S.S. *Michigan* which left her Great Lakes ways reluctantly, in privacy, but in good order in 1843, twenty years
before the *Monitor*.

The Navy did its best to forget her, history has practically
ignored her, and indeed, had not stalwart and faithful friends
fought doggedly and valiantly for her, there might not today
be a single reminder or relic of the ship that was not only the
Navy's first iron ship, but very likely its first prefabricated
vessel. It is a story in which shame is heaped upon shame,
insult upon insult, the recipient in every instance being the
ship that should have received the same respectful and devoted attention lavished, albeit belatedly, upon the *Constitution*. That she didn't receive it reflects a callous disregard

for fact, and emphasizes the scurrilous treatment she received at the hands of the service in which she should have been held in honored status—the U.S. Navy.

Twice robbed of her name, she lived on in misery and want after both her namesake successors had gone to the scrap pile. Yet, in Washington there were none to trumpet her cause, sing her praises, pinpoint her needs or succor her in her most dreadful hour of need. This was a ship that came no nearer than three hundred miles to saltwater, yet her very conception, building and existence exemplified the finest virtues of the service that later scorned her and cast her aside. Paradoxically, probably no other vessel of her size, a modest 164-feet, produced as many qualified sailors and distinguished officers as did the old U.S.S. *Michigan*. It is doubtful, too, that any other vessel fought so long and hard to live as did the "Old Girl," as they came to call her, in a career that stretched out over an incredible one hundred and six years.

In 1842 the Navy Department asked for plans for a barkentine-rigged, iron-hulled, shallow-draft, side-wheel steamer for use as a Great Lakes gunboat. The decision to build of iron was that of then Secretary of the Navy, A. P. Upshur. A dominant factor in the decision was, as he explained to some querulous members of Congress, "Giving as much aid as practicable in developing a new use for our immense national resources of the valuable metal, and secondly, to ascertain the practicability and utility of building vessels of so cheap and indestructible a material." The specifications, then, required that the hull should be of "American Juniata iron of the best quality."

A household word more than a century ago, this brand of iron, often known as wrought iron or charcoal iron, is not to be confused with what modern fabricators of railings and ornamental pieces call wrought iron, which is usually simple hot-rolled steel painted black. Juniata iron, famous for its toughness, durability and resistance to fractures, was produced in charcoal furnaces from ores found in Centre, Huntingdon and Mifflin counties, in central Pennsylvania.

Stackhouse and Tomlinson, of Pittsburgh, their plant now the site of the city's State Office Building, were the only bidders who proposed building the entire ship—hull, engines and boilers. Contrary to today's lamentable custom of pleas for contract "over-runs" and renegotiations, Stackhouse and Tomlinson agreed to build the vessel on a bid of thirteen and three-quarter cents per pound for the hull, and twenty-four cents per pound for the engines, "complete and erected in place."

After the iron plates, frames and bracing had been fabricated and numbered and the engine and boilers completed, the entire lot was shipped to the erection site, a small shipyard at the foot of French Street, in Erie, Pennsylvania. The combined mass of iron parts, 584 tons, went by Ohio River steamer to Chester, Pennsylvania, where it was reloaded on Ohio & Erie Canal boats for the long, slow trip to Cleveland. Here the load was transferred to lake vessels and, in several consignments, forwarded to Erie.

Mr. Samuel Hart, known popularly as the Gentlemanly Architect, had designed the U.S.S. *Michigan,* and, quite logically, was the man named to put the pieces together. The task proved to be an exasperating and enervating one. It changed Mr. Hart from a mild-mannered executive into a driving, demanding and frequently profane individual, often exhibiting the characteristics associated with third mates on

China clippers. A four-day trip from any iron foundry, he was compelled to choose and train his workmen and to forge his own tools. With no textbooks to guide him or experts to consult when problems arose, as they did daily, he developed physical and administrational skills not usually required of naval architects. About this time, too, the workers and many succeeding generations of crew and landlubbers dropped the formal "U.S.S." appellation, referring to her familiarly as the *Michigan*.

She was ready for launch on December 5, 1843, a savagely cold day. By agreement any of Erie's citizens who might be so disposed were invited to the launching. It was late in the afternoon when the last of the tallow had been applied to the ways, and other last-minute preparations made. Upon a signal from a gun all the church bells were to be rung. Shortly thereafter the *Michigan* would slide down into Erie Bay. The gun was fired, the bells rang and Mr. Hart raised an arm and dropped it, the signal to knock out the wedges that held the ship immobile. Then she began to move, the tallowed ways smoking from the weight while emitting a great groaning and creaking. The *Michigan,* however, moved only a third of her length before rumbling to a halt. She was stuck, hard and fast. Although the shipyard men energetically applied levers, ground tackle, massive improvised pry bars, and hammered more wedges with great diligence, the ship remained lifeless, inert—a great bulk seemingly frozen to the slippery ways that were to set her free forever on the freshwater seas, her intended destiny. With the coming of darkness Mr. Hart abandoned further efforts and with some embarrassment dismissed his men and indicated to the half-frozen spectators that the excitement was over for the day.

Mr. Hart did not sleep well that night, tossing restlessly and mentally reviewing the launching procedures, wondering where things had gone wrong. This unrest and worry resulted in his rising before dawn. Shivering, he wended his way to the shipyard. He walked through the gate, almost automatically avoiding the mounds of chocks, the tangle of ground tackle and piles of tools and cribbing. He raised his candle lantern to shoulder height so he could see the familiar bulk of the *Michigan*. She was not there! Frantically he picked his way over the debris to the very water's edge. There, very faintly, calmly at ease, like a contented cow in her pasture, could be seen the silhouette of the *Michigan,* trim and perfectly at home in Erie Bay. During the night the furious winds had done what a small army of workmen could not do with the sledges, blocks and wedges. They had given life to the *Michigan!*

Mr. Hart had really designed and built a most unusual ship. For despite her prototype status as the first iron ship of the U.S. Navy, she had a rather sharp, raking bow, such as characterized the clipper ships built years later, complete with graceful bowsprit, ornate billet head and trail boards. He was busy the next few months supervising the adjustments of her engine and installing armament and rigging. But before she could take her maiden voyage, unexpected developments drew her fangs and dulled her sting.

The *Michigan* was laid down to carry twelve guns to fire through deck ports and two sixty-eight pound Paixhans guns, mounted on swivels, one aft, the other on the fo'c'sle. Obviously this armament was the subject of much discussion in naval circles and inevitably word of such formidable firepower found its way to Mr. Packenham, the British Minister at Washington. Mr. Packenham, as it transpired, had a perfectly splendid memory, one which recalled a gentleman's agreement made some twenty-seven years earlier between Mr. Richard Rush, acting Secretary of State, and the Right Honorable Charles Bagot, His Brittanic Majesty's Minister Plenipotentiary to the United States of America. The gentleman's agreement, affirmed by a Presidential proclamation, very specifically limited armament on both Canadian and United States vessels plying the waters contiguous to both nations.

Mr. Packenham, alarmed at what seemed to him to be an outright violation of an agreement that had served perfectly as a treaty between the two countries, dashed off a strong protest to Mr. John C. Calhoun, our Secretary of State, pointing out that the United States had grossly violated the agreement by arming the *Michigan* with thirty-two-pound carronades and two sixty-eight-pound Paixhans guns instead of the one eighteen-pounder specified in the agreement.

Properly outraged at the oversight, Mr. Calhoun immediately sent a dispatch rider on his way to Erie with instructions that the *Michigan* was not to leave port until further orders had been received and acknowledged. What followed was a stern directive that the original fourteen guns be removed and replaced with a single eighteen-pounder. And that's all the *Michigan* carried on her first cruise and for many years thereafter.

Whatever her lack of firepower, the *Michigan* was unique in her economy of operation. One of her early skippers, Lieutenant Commander F. A. Roe, wrote to the Navy Department, "I have steamed 2492 miles and have consumed only 165 tons and 1283 pounds of soft coal. The *Michigan* is the most economical ship I ever knew, in fuel; she is a good steady ship and has cost the government less money than any other gunboat in its service."

Nine years after launching, the *Michigan* underwent top-side rebuilding. The rig was changed from barkentine to that of a topsail schooner. An enclosed chart house was built just forward of the paddle wheels, and a comfortable cabin was erected for the captain. It had the only bathtub on the ship.

The steam-driven paddle wheels, in the original concept, were to be employed primarily in maneuvering while entering or leaving port, or where traffic or adverse winds dictated. Otherwise she would use her sails. To prevent excessive drag when under way the wheels were stopped with a hand brake while a sailor climbed into the paddle-wheel boxes through a hatch and removed the lower paddles or "buckets."

If the sole criteria of naval history and subsequent honors are savage battles, heroic deeds and decks red with blood, the *Michigan* had no history of such. Only twice did she figure in events significant of public notice or mention in the news dispatches of the day.

The first occurred in 1851, on signed orders from the Secretary of the Navy. With Captain Bullis in command, the *Michigan,* after picking up U.S. District Attorney George Bates at Detroit, steamed to Beaver Island in upper Lake Michigan to arrest King James I, better known in mainland circles as James Jesse Strang. Strang, a Mormon who had found himself at odds with the church elders after spiritual leader Joseph Smith was assassinated, founded Mormon colonies in Illinois and Wisconsin before moving his flock, lock, stock and barrel, to Beaver Island, there to found a new "kingdom."

Absolute ruler and a stern one, Strang established a settlement known as St. James, which by 1851 numbered about seventeen hundred souls whose daily lives were regimented by their "king." There was, on the mainland, lively opposition to the colony, and everything from a fishing vessel "gone missing" to poor crops was attributed to "those damned Mormons." They were vilified, slandered and frequently brought to book on a variety of trumped-up charges and accused of crimes literally without substantiating evidence of any kind. They were the victims of suspicion, gossip and malicious rumors because of their religion, their austere existence and simply because they were "different."

But kingdom or no, Beaver Island was officially part of Michigan. Of the seventeen hundred Mormons about seven hundred were of voting age, enough in that period of time to swing the state into either the Whig or Democratic fold. President Millard Fillmore was keenly aware of this, hence the presence of U.S. District Attorney Bates aboard the *Michigan,* although the misdeeds for which King Strang was about to be arrested were too vague to justify the witness of a legal officer of such stature. Bates and armed deputies had warrants not only for Strang but for almost a score of his followers. All were brought aboard the *Michigan* for a hearing. The prosecution, however, could not provide credible evidence of any kind, and Bates had no choice but to turn the faithful free. But in view of his orders he insisted upon taking Strang back to Detroit for trial, not under arrest but "under surveillance." There Strang, a brilliant orator, so impressed the jury that he was exonerated, completely vindicated of any wrongdoing. It was only one of several instances in which he was brought before the courts on false and malicious charges.

The kingdom came to an end, as most eventually do, and this one because two women of the flock refused to wear long bloomers, as directed by their king. Unfortunately, their opposition to the orders was supported by their husbands, and this called for stern punishment. The two men were sentenced to be flogged the usual thirty-nine lashes. The deputies assigned to the task, in an outbreak of unusual religious zeal, doubled the dosage, inflicting such a beating that the pair were bedfast for days. They used the time to plot the downfall of their spiritual leader. Some time later, near the dock at St. James, they sprang at him from concealment, firing six shots into his chest. Then both assassins rushed to the sanctuary of the *Michigan,* which through fate or possible prearrangement just happened to be anchored nearby. They were taken to Mackinac and turned loose without charges being pressed, although King Strang died ten days later.

The Civil War found the *Michigan* guarding a Confederate prisoner-of-war camp on Johnson's Island, in Sandusky Bay, the Rush-Bagot agreement temporarily put aside or ignored. Midway in the conflict our relations with England were near the breaking point, and Confederate sympathizers were so numerous in Canada that guarding seventeen hundred prisoners with one gun was a farce. In November of 1863 the ship received additional armament—one thirty-pound Parrot Rifle, five twenty-pound rifles of the same type, eight howitzers, two twelve-pounders and six twenty-four pounders. She was bristling with firepower now, but with no place to go.

Twice she was the subject of Confederate plots to overcome her and free the prisoners, both schemes hatched in Canada. The first failed when one man informed the Canadian authorities, who immediately advised Washington. The second, much more involved, included simultaneous land and sea efforts and it is conceded by most historians to have come within twenty minutes of succeeding. This plot was belatedly made known to our government, too, but the information was incomplete. Hence they could do naught but wait, with the ship and her crew advised to be alert.

The plotters sent Captain Charles H. Cole, a Confederate officer, to Sandusky with orders to ingratiate himself with the *Michigan*'s officers and those in charge of the prison camp. He purported to be a Philadelphia banker and a staunch abolitionist who was, more incidentally, a jolly good fellow. He was the genial host at many parties at which champagne flowed freely and good entertainment was provided. At the prison camp which he visited, ostensibly out of compassion, he passed out treats and cigars to the prisoners. In the cigars, however, were tiny folded bits of paper giving instructions on what to do when the *Michigan* was captured. The plan included the prisoners forming an army which would immediately rush eastward to sack the cities of Sandusky, Lorain and Cleveland. The captured *Michigan,* meanwhile, would cruise offshore, bombarding the defenseless communities until the panic-stricken citizens fled in disorder. Then she would become a raider, disrupting supply lines to further demoralize the people.

The plot included seizure of the passenger steamer *Philo Parsons* which left Detroit on its scheduled daily run to Sandusky on September 21, 1864. Among the passengers was Bennett Burley, a seaman and Confederate spy. When the steamer stopped at Sandwich, Ontario, one of the boarding passengers was John Yates Beall, and at Amherstburg another stop a few miles away, more men came aboard carrying pistols and ammunition concealed in their luggage. At four o'clock on the morning of the twenty-second, Beall crept stealthily to the pilot house and put a pistol to the head of the first mate, informing him that the ship was now a prize of the Confederacy. Bennett Burley then took over the wheel. Later, near Lake Erie's Bass Islands, the *Island Queen,* still another steamer on the Sandusky-to-Detroit run, was overtaken. While Burley maneuvered the *Philo Parsons* alongside, Beall and several others jumped aboard the *Island Queen,* claiming it, too, as a prize of the Confederate States of America. But it sooned dawned upon Beall that he had insufficient manpower to control the prisoners on both vessels, so he put all but Captain Orr and his crew ashore on Middle Bass Island. Still later he decided that the *Island Queen* was a burden rather than a help, so after ordering the captain and crew aboard the *Philo Parsons,* he took measures to sink the *Island Queen* in deep water. But instead of sinking, the steamer drifted some miles away and finally grounded on Chickenolee Reef. The *Philo Parsons,* peopled now only by the raiding party and crews of the two vessels, steamed on toward Johnson's Island.

Meanwhile, Captain Cole, the "jolly good fellow," had arranged to entertain the *Michigan*'s officers at a banquet aboard ship, serving them champagne and wine, drugged for the occasion. When they were helpless, Cole was to fire a rocket, a signal for the simultaneous boarding and capture of the *Michigan* and rebellion by the Confederate prisoners at the camp.

The *Philo Parsons,* with the *Michigan* in sight, hove to off Cedar Point, backing and filling while awaiting the expected rocket. The signal never came because the captain of the *Michigan,* Commander J. C. Carter, had received the latest intelligence about Mr. Cole, the spurious Philadelphia banker with a penchant for giving champagne parties. He was immediately arrested and put in irons.

Aboard the *Philo Parsons* the furious Mr. Beall finally had to admit that somehow the plan had gone awry. He headed his captured vessel back to the Canadian shore where, after depositing the crew members in a marsh and getting his own men ashore, he set the steamer adrift.

Through her next forty years the *Michigan* served as an efficient training vessel, sending forth men whose names became household words when talk turned to the Navy and to bold deeds and action on the high seas. One of her commanders in early Civil War years was James E. Jouett, to whom, during the blazing attack on Mobile Bay, the famous Admiral Farragut addressed the immortal phrase, "Damn the torpedoes, Jouett, full speed ahead!"

Another of her illustrious sons was Charles V. Gridley. As commander of Admiral Dewey's flagship, the *Olympia,* he fired the first shot at Manila Bay after Dewey's quiet order, "You may fire when ready, Gridley!"

In 1905, when a host of Navy men and those who had served their time aboard the *Michigan* were already affectionately calling her the "Old Girl," the Navy snatched away her name, giving it to a new capital battleship, a vessel which, incidentally, the "Old Girl" was to outlive by two decades. In deference to the state for which she had originally been named, she was now designated the U.S.S. *Wolverine.*

In 1912 the Navy "turned over" the *Wolverine* to the Pennsylvania Naval Militia. During the next eleven years, under Commander William L. Morrison, she was a familiar sight all over the lakes as a training and survey vessel, staffed by members of the United States Naval Reserve. She visited all the American Great Lakes ports during World War I, as she had in the Spanish-American War, seeking out naval recruits. It is problematical how many Midwestern farm boys first felt the rolling of a deck aboard the *Wolverine,* but they would number in the thousands.

Always home-ported at Erie, the *Wolverine* hosted for training so many men who married Erie girls that the city was nicknamed "The Mother-in-Law of the U.S. Navy."

One thing the Navy didn't take away from her was a man who had been on her for seventeen years. Richard Coppar, a kindly, dignified black man, had been the captain's steward all that time. Coppar's most precious possession was his famous "wishing chair," a piece of furniture which apparently embodied mysterious powers. The chair had been given to him at Amherstburg, Ontario, when the ship had touched there during a good-will visit in the 1890s. Several events subsequently occurred which caused him to believe that the chair was possessed of the ability to make dreams or wishes come true for those who sat in it and "believed."

One day his daughter wrote unexpectedly, asking him for some money which, at the time, was in short supply. Moments after sitting in his chair while wondering what to do and wishing he had some money, Coppar went ashore on an errand. He had walked a scant twenty feet when he found eleven dollars on the dock. Other similar and unusual coincidences convinced him he had a truly remarkable chair. A generous fellow, he urged others to avail themselves of its magic. By 1910 he had five books filled with the names and addresses of those who had done so, and dozens of testimonials from people whose wishes had been fulfilled.

In August of 1923, in her seventy-ninth year, shortly after she had navigated the Straits of Mackinac and had hauled south on Lake Huron, the twenty-four-foot connecting rod on the *Wolverine*'s port cylinder snapped off three feet from the crank end, puncturing the cylinder head. It was not a defect after all these years, merely old age. She limped home to Erie at three miles per hour, blessed, fortunately, with good weather. Those who knew and loved her could almost feel her sigh of relief when strong hands moored her to familiar bollards.

It was assumed that the Navy, undoubtedly aware that its first iron ship, a historic treasure beyond price, was in mortal distress, would immediately authorize the modest sum required for necessary repairs. But sentiment did not weigh much on the balance scale of justice, and the Navy would not approve a dime for the "Old Girl's" refurbishing. Local groups pleaded in vain for her preservation as a historic vessel. It grew obvious as time went on, that the factor weighing most heavily against her was that her service, however honorable, had been on freshwater. This enigma of thought processes has always been baffling and frustrating to freshwater people.

Finally, in 1929, with docking space at a premium and the pleas of her friends still meeting stony silence, the *Wolverine* was moved from her moorings to a far corner of the bay, a portion appropriately called Misery Bay. It was here that Commodore Perry's flagship and other vessels of his gallant fleet were permitted to rot away and sink after the Battle of Lake Erie. A sturdy launch was secured for the towing job but scarcely proved adequate. The "Old Girl" seemed to know that her fate was sealed and began to show a dash of spirit, like the pathetic complaints of a protesting old matriarch being bundled off to the almshouse. Three times she took a sudden sheer to the north and open water, where she felt she belonged. Three times the hawser brought her up short, but on the third yank she swung around in a fit of temper and almost rammed the launch, missing it by inches. When she was finally pushed up on a mudbank, she petulantly kicked the launch up with her.

Steadfastly, as the years passed, her friends, still hoping for a miracle, petitioned Washington again and again to honor the historic vessel and participate in her preservation. It was a waste of time. At one time the Navy agreed to give the ship to the city of Erie, but later claimed that the gift was never formally accepted, a point hotly disputed by some prominent citizens. The Pennsylvania State Historical Commission flatly refused to give any financial aid. The Senate Committee on Naval Affairs was helpless. Navy red tape was seemingly insurmountable.

Pearl Harbor found the "Old Girl" still squatting ignominiously on the mudbank, defiant but deteriorating. In 1943 her friends had to take up the cudgels again, this time to keep the War Production Board from claiming her for scrap. Her wooden upper works had largely surrendered to the hot summer suns and bitter Erie winters, but her ironwork was still sound. And now her admirers had high hopes that President Roosevelt, a former Assistant Secretary of the Navy, might use his great influence to save her. But the President was busy running a war, and Washington's hundreds of brisk young naval officers had little time to spare for the old *Wolverine*.

It seems incredible that the helpless and historic old vessel should suffer even further indignities at the hands of the Navy, but that is exactly what happened. Late in 1942, with the submarine threat growing with each passing day and the need for carrier pilots critical, the Navy decided to convert two large Great Lakes passenger vessels, the *Greater Buffalo* and the *Seeandbee*, into practice and training aircraft carriers. The old *Greater Buffalo* became the U.S.S. *Sable* and the *Wolverine*'s name was taken from her for the *Seeandbee!* Now nameless, shamed and helpless, the first iron ship of the U.S. Navy became better known to her would-be benefactors as the orphan of Misery Bay. The practice aircraft carrier plan was never questioned since the two old passenger ships qualified 17,820 pilots for carrier duty, but surely the Navy could have found another name.

It wasn't until 1948 that a solution to the situation was discovered. Ironically, it had been the logical answer all through the quarter-century the old *Wolverine* had been embroiled in red tape. At the Navy Department, Captain Guilliott's secretary, with typical feminine directness, pointed out that under Public Laws of 1883 the Navy could sell the ship to a municipality or a non-profit corporation for cultural purposes by a negotiated sale with the President's approval.

President Truman, on June 22, 1948, signed his approval, and the gallant but neglected vessel became the property of The Foundation for the Preservation of the Original U.S.S. *Michigan*, Incorporated. The duly elected officers were Lieutenant Commander William L. Morrison (retired), long the

*Wolverine*'s commander; Herbert R. Spencer, a prominent Erie businessman; and attorney William B. Washbaugh. Spencer had been spearheading the campaign to save the ship for many years.

But now the old ship was, as an entity, far beyond the preservation stage. Her hull was partially filled with water and the cabins and upper works a decayed shambles. It was at once obvious that the cost of a complete restoration was out of the question. The only consideration now was how part of the famous old iron vessel could best be preserved for future generations.[2] It was decided finally that her bow and cutwater would be saved and mounted on a concrete base, complete with suitable landscaping and a plaque relating her history. Funds for this would become available with the sale of the balance of the hull for scrap.

Getting the now nameless hulk to the breaker's yard was more of a task than the purchaser had bargained for, and the operation amused the aged ship's friends no end. The "Old Girl," now that the worst had come, was adamant. What should have been a three-day effort in dragging her off the mudbank into deep water took four weeks. The water inside her proved to be only that accumulated in rains. Her hull was as sound as it had been in 1843. They lightened her by torching off the paddle wheels and removing other heavy gear. Still, she clung to her moorings in the mud with great resolve and tenacity. Finally, late one afternoon they got her free, but too late in the day to move her to her scrapping dock. Word got around that the next day would see the final, fateful voyage. There were many people watching when the launch hooked up the towline, some of them misty-eyed men who had sailed on her. They all knew that she had a personality of her very own and were delighted when she unleashed her last spasm of wrath at her tormentors by ramming and sinking the towing launch. But she was quick to repent, which was her true nature, by promptly picking up the drenched launch crew. Throughout it all she never lost her dignity, floating proudly there in the bay, trim, beautiful and reposed, flaunting her lovely clipper-ship lines that were decades ahead of the saltwater ships that followed her.

But even the revenue from the hull, as scrap, was not enough to provide the desired and fitting last resting place for the bow and cutwater. Herbert R. Spencer himself removed many items in the scrapping stage, things that were then offered by the Foundation as souvenirs, at modest cost. Rivets were forged into letter openers, appropriately inscribed with the name and launching date of the old U.S.S. *Michigan.* Bolts, spikes, bars, valve handles, small castings, sister hooks and even the scrimshawed brass sheets that decorated the engine cylinders were offered and sold. The total yield from scrap and souvenirs was $2,432, all of which was used in erecting the raking bow, to sailors still a thing of true beauty. Commander Morrison had offered the rare old tandem compound engine to the Smithsonian Institution, but it was rejected. Once again the Pennsylvania State Historical Commission refused assistance. When curious workmen gauged the hull plates, they found that deterioration was absolutely zero, a splendid tribute to early American iron makers and Juniata iron!

She sits there now, erect and proud in the park at the foot of Erie's State Street, a stone's throw from the rebuilt and refurbished *Niagara,* Commodore Perry's flagship, looking out over Erie Bay to the open waters she knew so intimately for almost eighty years. Only one other ship's bow is so preserved and displayed, the H.M.S. *Vindictive*, at Zeebrugge, Belgium.

And if there is a slightly elevated rake to her cutwater, billet head and bowsprit, one can only conclude that it constitutes a sniff of contempt for the government that treated her so shabbily.

---

[1] Like the U.S.S. *Michigan*, the *Constitution* had more close calls at the hands of the Navy than from enemy action. Built in 1797 she served until 1830 when, after decommissioning, the Navy proposed breaking her up. But a young poet, Oliver Wendell Holmes, aroused the sympathy of the entire nation with his poem "Old Ironsides." Reluctantly, the Navy rebuilt her and she stayed on active duty until 1882, like the U.S.S. *Michigan* primarily as a training vessel for naval officers and seamen recruits.

In 1905 the Navy proposed using her for target practice and again an outraged country protested. By 1925 she was again in such sad shape that a nationwide campaign was needed to raise restoration funds. Much of it came from school children who contributed $500,000 in nickels, dimes and pennies. Then Congress, shamed into action, coughed up the balance of the amount needed. Altogether the *Constitution* has had six major rebuildings in her 177-year career. And now, in a highly unusual expression of sentiment, Congress has appropriated funds to assure her a safe voyage into still another century.

[2] The mainmast of our nation's first iron naval vessel now serves as the flag pole at the Fairport Harbor Marine Museum, in Fairport Harbor, Ohio. The museum itself was once the home of the lighthouse keeper who tended the adjoining lighthouse, built in 1825, rebuilt in 1871, and still one of the museum's unusual exhibits. The museum is operated by the Fairport Harbor Historical Society.

# 4

## "Ma's Out There . . . Somewhere"

Sailing-vessel masters had many occupational crosses to bear, not the least of which were adverse winds, contrary currents and utter helplessness in flat calms. They overcame the first by superb seamanship, minimized the second by an intimate knowledge of the waters they sailed, and the last by exercising extreme patience. But there was one unpredictable and devilishly capricious freak of weather they could do nothing about—the phenomenon known as the white squall.[1]

White squalls were and are as common on saltwater as freshwater, respecting no sea, latitude, hemisphere or season. As yet unexplained by meteorological science, they are stealthy, sudden and violent—whirlwind-like tempests which seem to spring from nowhere to maul and buffet their victims, briefly but frequently fatally. There is no visual clue or discernible evidence such as darkening skies, mounting seas or lowering clouds. Obviously then, there is no defense against the unforeseen. They strike day or night, under ideal sailing conditions, furiously twisting manifestations that some of nature's secrets have yet to be probed or revealed.

Understandably then, they were a major concern before the transition to steam, and undoubtedly many vessels, from the schooners of the Great Lakes to the big tea clippers of the deep seas, have "gone missing" from unknown causes when, in all truth, the probability was that some were overtaken and overwhelmed by that unseen scourge, the white squall. Steamers would be little affected beyond a rude cuffing about and the loss of loose gear and dignity. A laden Great Lakes schooner with her canvas up would likely be shorn of her sails, shrouds, stays and masts, possibly blown over on her beam ends to lie there helpless in the trough, prey for whatever winds and seas later developed. But the schooner devoid of cargo was the most vulnerable victim. Completely without bulk and weight low in her holds to counteract the skulking but invisible enemy, she would likely as not be capsized immediately. In the vernacular of those who survived such catastrophic maulings, the experience was described as being "knocked-down."

What but a white squall could explain the 1875 loss of the staunch *Rosa Belle,* discovered floating upside down in Lake Michigan by a Pere Marquette carferry? Captain Ehrhardt Geise and his crew of nine were missing and never found. Four years earlier, in 1871, although carrying a full load of coal for Chicago, the brig *Mechanic,* Captain Henry McKee in command, was suddenly struck down with all hands, again in Lake Michigan. During the same season the schooner *New Lisbon* was knocked-down on Lake Erie, going down near Fairport where earlier the bark *Sunshine* had similarly capsized with most of her crew lost. An odd happenstance occurred in June of 1872 when the schooner *Jamaica,* Captain David Bothwell in charge, sailed from Milwaukee. She was caught in a white squall on Lake Huron, capsizing instantly. Fortunately the crew were on deck and, although pitched into the water, were soon rescued by the crew of the schooner *Starlight*. Strangely enough, she had suffered the same fate the year before at almost the same spot.

A white squall was suspected in the disappearance of the big schooner *Thomas Hume* which departed Chicago on the evening of May 21, 1891, and was never sighted again. The theory was even more plausible when it was learned that the *Hume* was light and, when last observed, had every inch of her canvas up. On the other hand, a full cargo is probably what saved the schooner *Naiad*. Heavily burdened with coal for Chicago, the *Naiad* was off Charlevoix in July of 1895 when she was struck by a white squall. Although two of her crew were lost and the schooner dismasted and left virtually a floating wreck, the coal cargo prevented her from capsizing. A lumber cargo, however, did not prevent the schooner *L. B. Shepard* from flipping bottom side up, and with good reason. Operators in the lumber trade consistently hauled impressive deck cargoes, sometimes as much as they carried in the holds. Thus the lumber-laden sailing vessels were almost always top-heavy and easily knocked-down in a sudden blow of any magnitude. And the *L. B. Shepard,* all her canvas displayed, was no exception.

The meteorological factors that spawned white squalls were as much a mystery in the 1800s as they are today. Also inexplicable are those sudden and devastating localized gales that manifest themselves in quickly forming squalls with observable characteristics. These usually develop and sweep on with such swiftness that even the most alert mariner has little or no time to prepare for them, let alone take evasive action. In the broad weather fronts that could be tracked and foreseen by the weather experts of the time, squalls, white or otherwise, were the unpredictable mavericks, the arch-enemy who lurked, often unseen even on the fairest day, to pounce from ambush upon the unwary and unprepared wind ship.

How many schooners, brigs and barks fell victim to white squalls or the mauling of severe, fast-forming localized gales that struck quickly and dissipated almost as swiftly is anybody's guess. Many such craft, capsized and beaten down, simply vanished. Others left traces in the form of wreckage or of survivors who were forevermore in awe of these weather eccentricities, as they were in awe of anything of which they did not have knowledge. Over the years such calamities sank or left wrecked or capsized an amazing armada of vessels, many of them losing all or part of their people. Struck down on Lake Michigan were the schooners *Gallinipper, Ontonagon, Lewis C. Irwin, L. M. Hubly, William Foster, Ellen Pine, Blue Bell, J. A. Davis, E. B. Ward, W. R. Hanna, Stella, Spray, Maggie Thompson, Silver Cloud, Dawn, James D. Sawyer* and the *City of Toledo.*

On Lake Erie such undetected conspiracies of the elements conquered the brig *Cuyahoga,* the bark *B. A. Standart* and the schooners *T. G. Colt, A. L. Hazelton, A. E. Marsilliot, Australia, Josephine, North Star* and *H. A. Lamars.*

On Lake Ontario the clandestine winds, meeting in torment, struck down the bark *E. H. Rae* and the schooners *William Penn* and *Fleetwind* and the brig *Olivia,* the well-known Captain Bradbeer in command.

Communications such as we know today were nonexistent. News of interest to mariners on the Great Lakes usually came from other mariners, relayed via ship chandlers' supply boats, and from tugmen who towed them through the connecting river or simply shouted from one deck to another as upbound and downbound vessels passed. Warnings of a recent wreck that might be a navigational hazard, requests to be on the watch for a missing boat or her crew and other pertinent information were by word of mouth, but highly effective. And all too often the news was that the hull of an unknown vessel, possibly overtaken by a treacherous white squall, was floating about at the will of the wind and that a sharp watch should be kept to avoid collision.

For good reason, then, the onset of the one thing he could not anticipate or prevent, the white squall, was a forever lingering worry to the concerned and conscientious shipmaster, already burdened with the details of navigation, the well-being of his vessel and the interests of his crew and owner. For he knew that the most astute, experienced and weather-wise skipper, however long he held command, was helpless in the face of an invisible adversary who attacked without the usual warning of glowering skies or sharply dropping barometer.

Such a shipmaster was Captain Fred Sharpsteen of Sebewaing, Michigan, master of the twenty-year-old, two-masted schooner *Hunter Savidge*. In the spring of 1899, when he went to Alpena to fit out the schooner, as had been his responsibility for a considerable number of years, he left behind in Sebewaing his beloved wife Rosa, whom he and his sons affectionately called "Ma." At home Ma was the skipper, ruling with a firm but kindly hand that had earned the adoration of her brood, the gentle matriarch who ran a taut but happy ship. But this spring was different, in that, while young David stayed at home with Ma, the captain took with him his sixteen-year-old son, John, to sign on as a crew member. Methodical and cautious, Captain Sharpsteen was in the employ of lumber entrepreneur John Muellerweiss, Jr., who also owned the schooners *Glad Tidings* and *Herschell.* Mr. Muellerweiss kept the three vessels as busy as possible, but with the lumber business being what it was with seasonal ups and downs, he was inclined to find cargoes, whatever they might be and wherever they were offered. The *Hunter Savidge* had been built in Grand Haven, Michigan, by the Savidge family, prominent in the lumbering business. Mrs. Savidge's maiden name had been Hunter, hence the name of the schooner. Her name was also carried on a tug used to maneuver log rafts to the mill dock and assist schooners and steamers at the Savidge dock in Manistee Harbor, Michigan, on the Upper Peninsula.

The schooner, before or after being acquired by Mr. Muellerweiss, had not been a particularly lucky vessel nor, for that matter, did she have an unusual affinity to mishaps, the lone exception being in 1892 while under the command of Captain Benjamin McCaffrey. She had blundered into the schooner *Minnie Davis,* sinking her immediately. Mr. Muellerweiss had been assessed the damages done to the *Minnie Davis* and also ordered to pay the value of the coal cargo lost in the collision. Beyond this incident the schooner was known as a staunch craft which more than once had "shown the way" to steamers when she had the right wind.

Nor had the *Glad Tidings* been entirely free of the trials and tribulations inherent to sailing vessels. In 1874, when she was being sailed by Captain George Hanson, he had made the mistake of crossing the bow of the steamer *Pathfinder,* near Grassy Island, in the approaches to Green Bay harbor, sinking the schooner. Fortunately she went down in shallow water and was soon salvaged, but not without the usual claims and counterclaims that seasoned the life and elevated the blood pressure of owners.

Under the management of Mr. Muellerweiss the *Hunter Savidge* had carried varied cargoes. On one voyage under Captain McCaffrey her holds had housed equipment for a northern lumbering operation he was interested in—camp gear, stoves, work horses and hundreds of bales of hay. Fortunately the weather had been good and Captain McCaffrey, after making sure the holds were swept clean of the droppings and spilled oats, hurried back to the Muellerweiss dock in Alpena to load lumber for Toledo. Despite these occasional "institutional" voyages the schooner had an enviable reputation as a money maker and smart sailer.

The afternoon of Sunday, August 20, 1899, found the *Hunter Savidge* some six miles off Pointe aux Barques, on Lake Huron, homeward bound to Alpena after what, in the life of a schooner, would be considered a humdrum voyage with but one exception—it was one of the few times she had ever carried passengers. Captain Sharpsteen had his dear Ma aboard for the trip, her first. Sharing the cabin with her were Mrs. Muellerweiss and her six-year-old daughter, Henrietta, known to friends, family and neighbors simply as Etta. Mr. Muellerweiss did not normally approve of having his family aboard one of his vessels, but an exception had been made because his wife, Mary, had not been feeling well and it was thought she might benefit from such a voyage, free of the distractions and responsibilities ashore. Ma Sharpsteen was making the journey to provide company for her. The crew consisted of young John Sharpsteen, first mate Thomas Doby and seamen Charles Cook, George Ellery, Ed Beal and George Francis. Cook, fittingly enough, was the ship's cook, but he took his place on deck when his services were required.

The *Hunter Savidge* had departed Alpena on August 3, bound for Detroit with 10,000 cedar posts. The trip was uneventful except for some unloading problems in Detroit where the posts had to be unloaded by hand. From Detroit the schooner sailed to Cleveland where Mr. Muellerweiss had managed to charter a coal cargo for Sarnia, Ontario, at the southern tip of Lake Huron. The ladies had enjoyed some sightseeing in both Cleveland and Detroit, and Ma was duly impressed with the big cities. Beyond the usual "bituminous dandruff" that sullied the decks and seemed to find its way into every nook and cranny of the cabin, the coal cargo had been disposed of briskly. Captain Sharpsteen did not like coal dust and as soon as the schooner had made sail he had his crew busy with the water buckets and brooms. The return trip to Alpena promised to be a short and pleasant one, but he knew, as all skippers did, that a sailing vessel without cargo was extremely vulnerable to strong and sudden winds. He confided to his son that he "would be very happy when the ladies are ashore."

The winds had been light enough all the way up the lake from Sarnia, but at about four o'clock off Pointe aux Barques they died completely. It was oppressively hot, hazy and muggy as the *Hunter Savidge* lay motionless on the water, utterly becalmed, her canvas hanging gray and limp, ready to catch any errant breeze that might spring up. Earlier Captain Sharpsteen had expressed high hopes of being home in Alpena by noon the next day, but that possibility now seemed very remote. The ladies—Mary Muellerweiss, little Etta and

Ma—were resting in the cabin. Noises in the galley indicated that Mr. Cook, with a fine show of energy, was making his preparations for the evening meal. Young John Sharpsteen, in heavy rubber boots, was sluicing the last of the coal dust into the scupper with the help of seamen Ellery, Beal and Francis. Mate Doby was busy with other chores and lanky Captain Sharpsteen languished hopefully at the wheel, fingering his mustache, wiping his brows and eagerly searching the skies for a weather sign that would indicate a bit of wind in the offing.

The *Hunter Savidge* was a sitting duck for the white squall that seemingly came booming from nowhere, an insane, twisting sledge-hammer wind that came on without a warning sound or visible evidence until it was upon the subservient schooner. When it hit, the banshee winds were terrifying. With all her canvas up, the *Hunter Savidge* was anything but the immovable object struck by an irresistible force. The sudden explosion of wind force drove her ahead, spun her around and pounded her bow deep down below the surface, at the same time rolling her over on her beam ends amid a wild cacophony of sails finally blowing out like cannon shot and the deathly whirring and snapping of parting shrouds, lines and chains. It was all over in ten seconds, and beyond a couple of enormous eruptions of air which burst upward from her empty hold, the schooner was on the same languid seas that had becalmed her. She had rolled completely over and was again right side up, but now only her extreme stern and about forty feet of her topmast were above water. The vessel, suspended at a rakish angle, was afloat only because of air trapped in the after section of the hull and possibly in her cabins. It was suddenly quiet again except for the thrashing of those thrown in the water and their cries to each other.

Captain Sharpsteen found himself in the water beside his schooner. A few feet away was his son John, trying to hang on to part of a wooden ladder. But his heavy rubber boots and an entanglement of loose cordage dragged him down. In seconds, within almost an arm's reach of his father, he was gone. Just then Charles Cook popped to the surface, blowing like a whale. His mad underwater thrashings had broken a galley window through which he escaped. Captain Sharpsteen grabbed Cook and helped him find a hand-hold on the rudder. There they were joined by George Ellery, Ed Beal and George Francis, all of whom had been on deck at the time the twisting white squall struck. The captain, hoping that like Cook, the ladies had somehow found an escape route, kept calling hoarsely, "Ma, Ma, where are you, Ma?" Mate Doby, burdened by heavy boots like John Sharpsteen, never surfaced. There they clung, the five survivors, surrounded by the debris from the *Hunter Savidge*—dunnage timbers, hatch cover planking and a smattering of flotsam that included the captain's uniform cap.

Fortunately, the wheelsman on the distant and upbound steamer *McVittie* had witnessed the schooner being knocked-down and in fifteen minutes she was alongside and launching a yawl boat. From the vantage point of the steamer's deck Captain Sharpsteen anxiously scanned the waters in search of Ma and the Muellerweiss ladies. There was not a sound, but the *Hunter Savidge* still hung there, her stern pointing up at an angle of forty-five degrees, a flag hanging limply from the protruding mast.

Captain Sharpsteen would have preferred to linger on the

site to explore the wreck just in case the air pocket which kept his vessel barely afloat also existed in the cabin where Ma, Mary Muellerweiss and little Etta might still be alive. But the captain of the *McVittie* was a strange, unsympathetic soul. He insisted that no life could remain on the almost submerged schooner and that he must continue his trip with no more delay. To that end he signaled the downbound steamer *H. E. Runnels* and transferred his passengers. The *Runnels,* he pointed out, would pass near Sand Beach (now Harbor Beach), a harbor of refuge where a United States Lifesaving Service Station would be in a better position to offer assistance and a thorough search of the wreck. Despite approaching darkness the compassionate master of the *Runnels* ordered up all possible speed and, as his vessel neared the breakwater entrance, blew distress signals to alert the lifesavers. The station crew hurried the shipwrecked mariners to their snug quarters, plied them with spirits and provided dry clothing. Keeper H. D. Ferris, enmeshed in red tape like all government workers, was required to note and account for any supplies doled out to unfortunate sailors. He duly noted disbursements: two pairs of pants, one pair of shoes, two overshirts, two pairs of drawers, three pairs of socks, four cardigan jackets, four handkerchiefs and one undershirt. The spirits consumed came under a different category, supplies used from the station's medicine chest.

While some of the lifesavers were out trying to locate a local diver he had requested, Captain Sharpsteen, beside himself with worry and grief, paced the station grounds, muttering at the delay and mentally promising Ma that he would be back for her soon. In his own mind he had convinced himself that his Ma, Mary Muellerweiss and little Etta could very possibly be still alive, trapped in a cabin air pocket just like the one that was keeping the stern of the schooner afloat, and all the while calling down anathemas upon him for deserting them.

Futile, fanciful and desperate though the captain's hope might be, there was certainly precedence and substance to his theory in the oft-told and true sailor stories of just such happenings—people given up for dead but provided with life and support by air trapped within a hull or cabin in a sudden capsizing. Drawing on his memory to bolster his seemingly hopeless theory and sustain his spirits, he could recall some notable instances. A case in point was that of Mrs. Napier, trapped in a lower cabin with her children when a sudden and fierce storm had capsized the schooner *Experiment*, leaving the vessel upside down on the bar off St. Joseph, Michigan, anchored there by the stubs of her broken masts. When curious boatmen visited the wreck the next day and were clumping around on the schooner's bottom they heard a faint pounding and strange noises within the hull. Quickly axes were provided, and when they had chopped a hole through the heavy planking, they lifted out Mrs. Napier and two of her children. They were alive simply because of air trapped in their cabin as the *Experiment* flipped over.

And there was the time when the schooner *Jane* capsized quickly one night off Little Point Sable. The captain was alone at the wheel when the squall struck and was thrown overboard. But he clambered back on the wreck, dove down to the cabin and rescued his two sons who had been asleep.

But the most remarkable such event had taken place some years earlier and was also utterly true, vouched for by some of the most respected men in the industry, including the well-known Captain Appleby, a prominent lower-lakes skipper and vessel owner, for whom it had been a personal experience. Part owner of the schooner *New Connecticut,* Captain Appleby, of Conneaut, Ohio, had put an aunt aboard the vessel, bound for Buffalo. The captain was engaged in the building of the new steamer *North American* and had urged her to wait until the steamer was completed, but anxious to return home to her family, she was adamant. Hence, Captain Appleby had no qualms about putting her aboard the *New Connecticut,* knowing that the master and crew would give her every consideration. All was well until the schooner passed Erie, Pennsylvania, when a sudden squall rolled her over on her starboard side, almost but not quite upside down. The cabins were totally under water. The crew hastily cut loose the yawl boat and, presuming the lady had drowned, pulled for shore and made their way back to Conneaut. Three days later Captain Appleby sought the aid of a friend, Captain Wilkins of the steamer *William Peacock,* which was bound for Buffalo, in locating the wreck and recovering the body of his aunt.

Captain Wilkins was successful in finding the *New Connecticut* and put first mate William Henton aboard the wreck to search. The schooner was still far over on her starboard side, the cabin still submerged and the vessel apparently almost full of water. Mate Henton probed in the cabin with a pike pole for some time, poking in what he thought was every nook and corner of it. When no body was forthcoming, the conclusion was drawn that the lady, adamant as ever, had floated out into the lake. Further search was abandoned. Two days later Captain Appleby himself sought out the wreck with equipment to right the hull and tow her to a nearby port for a thorough pumping out. When the *New Connecticut* had been almost completely righted, the "drowned" aunt, mustering what dignity she could salvage from the situation, walked through waist-deep water and up to the deck where she collapsed in the arms of the good Captain Appleby. Sailors cried out, and her son who had come to help wept unashamedly. She had been in the cabin five days and nights, most of the time with water almost up to her shoulders. She could not lie down and cat-napped while standing. Her only food had been a cracker and an onion, floating in from the galley supplies. She had heard the earlier boarding party and saw the pike pole sweeping her quarters. But she was afraid and didn't realize that it was a means of escape. She reported that she had repeatedly called out, asking if she was supposed to grasp the pole, but her cries were unheard by mate Henton. Captain Appleby, a deeply religious man, told the story wherever his voyages took him, always citing it as "a God's miracle."

These were the agonizing thoughts and haunting possibilities that wracked the mind of Captain Sharpsteen as he paced to and fro on the beach at the lifesaving station. He had requested the services of a diver to probe the submerged cabin of the *Hunter Savidge* for signs of life and, if this were not to be so, to recover the bodies. But the diver, located by the lifesavers and despite the captain's fervent pleas, refused to go out at night, saying it would be next to impossible to work under water in the dark.

Captain Sharpsteen, bone-weary, threw himself down on a bed to rest, but found sleep impossible. Finally, at two o'clock in the morning he roused two of the lifesaving crew who, noting his overwrought condition and getting a consenting nod from keeper Ferris, agreed to accompany him on a search in the station's small boat. For the rest of the night they cruised back and forth in the area where the captain was certain the *Hunter Savidge* still floated with only her stern above water. But the search in the dark was fruitless. At dawn they were joined by the station's larger boat, Captain Frank Lillis in the tug *Frank W.*, and the lifeboat from the Pointe aux Barques lifesaving station. The sympathetic crews crossed and crisscrossed a wide expanse of sea where the schooner should have been had she continued to float. At noon Captain Sharpsteen, his head bowed and his face haggard and tear-stained, regretfully concluded that further efforts would be in vain. Ma was gone!

Back at the station poor Captain Sharpsteen who, like many of his following, had been offered little opportunity for formal schooling beyond the first few grades, nevertheless penned a poignant note to his surviving son, David:

Sand Beach  Aug. 22  99

Dear Son David you are all I have in this world to help me morn for our Dear ones we have lost. I've been trying to locate the Reck to get Ma but John drowned while hanging to some steps. I think he was first for if he could have swam ten feet I could have saved him. I saved Cook and sailor with oil coat. I pulled them on the Reck. You will get the hole Particulars which I rote last night. You tell Sluchter to deliver letter to Charley Hemerline or you take it up soon as you can. I have got to go to Alpena soon as I give up looking for the schr. I lost every thing I've got, I've got a pair of Pants and old Shoes and Sowwestern that is all I have to my name but what the folks give me. I will write more soon I Remain your Pa as ever

F. Sharpsteen

Suddenly, two days later, came news to the station that the propeller *Shenango* had sighted the wreck on the day following the accident but at a point somewhat south of Pointe aux Barques. Again the tugs went charging out from Sand Beach, just too late to learn of the telegram that had arrived at the lifesaving station from Port Huron. The message related that the wreckage sighted had been that of the schooner *Brenton,* lost two months earlier.

Barely had the searching boats returned to Sand Beach when the fishing tug *Cassie M.* arrived carrying the *Hunter Savidge*'s yawl. More reports came from other vessels, most of them asserting that they had sighted the schooner, still afloat four days after the white squall. Again the captain took up the almost hopeless search, joined once more by friends in the tugs *Angeles* and *Sand Beach,* their crews seeking only to oblige the haggard and desperate man. Between searches on the lake Captain Sharpsteen walked miles along the beach north of Sand Beach, fearing that the wreck had drifted inshore where her low, almost completely submerged profile would be lost against the background of land by those in the boats. To those who encountered his now-gaunt figure and sought to comfort him he was gentle enough but seemingly too preoccupied to understand, merely mumbling, "Ma's out there . . . somewhere."

Still later the schooner's water casks were picked up and delivered to the lifesaving station, triggering another fruitless combing of the waters. Subsequently the schooner *Herschell,* another Muellerweiss vessel, reported finding planking from the *Hunter Savidge,* but it was loose material used to protect the deck while loading.

Captain Sharpsteen, nearing physical collapse from lack of

sleep and only an occasional bit to eat, still paced the beach constantly, his red-rimmed eyes always out on Lake Huron, a tall haunting figure seeking Ma and another of "God's miracles."

Back in Alpena, when word of the disaster became known, the whole town was shocked and went into mourning, flags flying at half-mast. Mr. Muellerweiss, utterly distraught and frantic with grief, was in such a depressed mood that friends watched him carefully, fearing that he might do himself harm. It was felt that only the knowledge of the three teen-age children he had left kept him from throwing himself into the black waters of Thunder Bay. And tempers in Alpena, when the details of the disaster became known, rose to the boiling point, the anger being directed at the captain of the *McVittie*. In the opinion of those who heard the official accounts, he had been extremely callous and offhand in his actions in quickly departing the scene of the wreck, turning the unfortunate survivors over to another vessel so as not to delay his own schedule. The *Alpena Argus* saw fit to express the mood of the community editorially:

> Alpena citizens are loud in the disapproval of the manner in which the captain of the steamer *McVittie* abandoned the wreck, and should he ever visit this city he will be called upon to explain his actions which are generally regarded as cowardly or brutal, in not making an attempt to recover the bodies or at least towing the wreck into shallow water.

But time, as they are prone to say, is a healer of all wounds. Captain Fred Sharpsteen, after returning in grief to his native Sebewaing, soon went back to the only trade he knew and was subsequently "converted" to steam, serving as master of several large and powerful steamers. Meanwhile, as the years passed, the tragic story of the *Hunter Savidge* and her gaunt and tormented captain walking the beach became a favorite and oft-repeated legend and fo'c'sle yarn. And many sailors, having an affinity for the bizarre and the juice of the grape, were wont to think they had sighted the ghostly stern of the *Hunter Savidge,* sliding by in the wraith-like fogs on Lake Huron, still suspended like a puppet by the air trapped in her hull and cabins and moving about at the whim of the winds and currents. Such apparitions were reported many times over the years but were quickly discounted as the hallucinations of superstitious and imaginative men.

Captain Sharpsteen later remarried and fathered two more sons. He still earned his living aboard a vessel and in command. Yet whatever boat was his, the crew was cognizant of the fo'c'sle sagas about the *Hunter Savidge* and were sympathetic to the man who had walked endless miles along the lonely shore hoping vainly for a miracle. They noticed, too, that when his boat was traversing Lake Huron, particularly near Pointe aux Barques, that the captain rarely was quiet, pacing the bridge or deck with a furrowed brow, his anxious, restless eyes scanning the blue waters. They knew, too, that Captain Fred Sharpsteen, subconsciously perhaps, but in his own way, was still searching. For "Ma" was still out there, somewhere.

[1] Savage squalls, springing seemingly from nowhere, are as common today as in the era of sail. On August 10, 1971, Captain Kurth Grainger of the steamer *Peter Reiss* notified the Cleveland Weather Service by radio-telephone of a sudden Lake Erie squall which, although it lasted only seven minutes, spawned winds of up to one hundred miles per hour.

# 5

A Witches' Brew — The Devil's Harvest

SUNDAY, NOVEMBER 10, 1940, was a seasonal jewel over most of the Midwest—a warm, clear day of bright sun and a soft, easterly wind, possibly the last installment on what had been a delightful period of Indian summer. It was the kind of day for a drive in the country, a walk along the beach, for raking leaves or a final woodland hike. It was the kind of day when most people wanted to be outdoors and followed their inclinations. Best of all was the fact that Monday also promised to be balmy for the holiday, Armistice Day, November 11, the day the great war to end wars had come to an end exactly twenty-two years earlier. Yet, even as the unseasonal temperatures belied the calendar, war was again raging in Europe. Besieged England was fighting for her very survival and pleading for help. France had already fallen and the Germans had invaded Denmark and Norway. On that enchanting Sunday in mid-America, it was almost as if those who were enjoying it were subconsciously fearful that this might be the last of such carefree days.

Out on the lakes the crewmen of many vessels, knowing

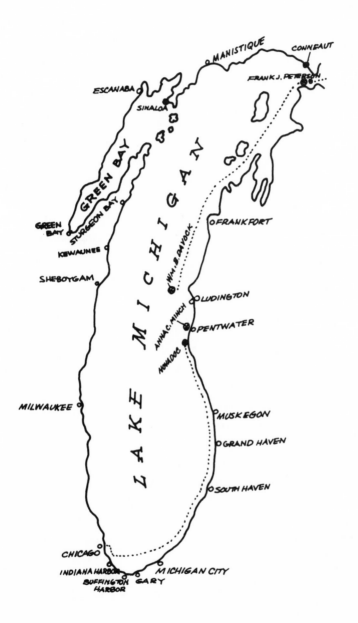

full well what treacherous weather November usually brought, took advantage of one of nature's rare autumn blessings—yarning, writing letters home or just basking in the sun. Over shipboard radios the war news was exciting and ominous. President Roosevelt, just re-elected to his third term, had already arranged to trade Great Britain fifty over-age destroyers for long leases on strategic naval and air bases. The Luftwaffe was pounding Coventry, the RAF was fighting valiantly and the world was still electrified by Prime Minister Churchill's "Blood, Sweat and Tears" speech. On the home front, thanks to production of military hardware for our beleaguered friends, the economy was beginning to boom. It appeared, too, that the Chicago Bears and the Washington Redskins would inevitably clash in the National Football League playoff.

They went about their business, the long lake vessels of both Canadian and U.S. fleets—tankers, crane boats, straight-deckers and self-unloaders, all deep-bellied with badly needed cargoes of raw materials to produce the armament which would in a matter of months, be supplied as part of a vast lend-lease program. Coal, iron ore, oil, limestone, sulfur, grain and scrap were in great demand and moving in astronomical tonnages. The grim days of the 1930s were over and thanks to rock-bottom scrap prices that prevailed during the Great Depression, there were still plenty of bottoms around to carry the urgent burdens to the heavy industry centers of Chicago, Gary, Indiana Harbor, Detroit, Lorain, Toledo, Cleveland and Buffalo. By now more and more patriotic orators were referring to the whole lower lakes area as "The arsenal of democracy," just as they had during World War I.

But neither those afloat nor ashore, reveling in the unseasonable temperatures on that November 10, could have been expected to evince much interest in such professional weather terminology as barometric minima, temperature height-curves, isotropic charts, radiosonde observations, tropopause, troposphere, kinetic energy or millibars. This was the jargon of weather-bureau experts, and in the bureau's fourteenth-floor offices in Chicago's United States courthouse, all these technical considerations were sinister factors shaping up on the synoptic maps to indicate the most unusual and awe-inspiring weather situation those on the bureau's Sunday staff had ever encountered.

Three days earlier, on November 8, a tremendous low-pressure system off the coast of Washington began moving inland. Accompanying it were cyclonic winds so fierce the Tacoma Narrows bridge swayed and swung ominously and then collapsed. At the same time another low-pressure disturbance far to the south crossed the Rocky Mountains and curved eastward over the southern Great Plains, encountering a broad flow of warm, moist Gulf air over the central Mississippi Valley before veering north-northeast over the extreme upper Mississippi Valley and upper Great Lakes. With the southernmost front now swinging northward like a giant scythe to meet the arctic front still booming along and sweeping over the northern plains states, warmer air, trapped between the fronts, promoted and encouraged a circular, counter-clockwise pattern to what was, moment by moment, becoming a massive cyclonic storm covering thousands of square miles, possibly the worst in a century.

In the weather bureau offices worried men watched the data coming in on the teletype machines from a score of reporting stations, constantly updating the synoptic map

of menacing forces. They could chart the courses of the con-
verging fronts accurately but they could not possibly predict
with a reasonable degree of certainty the intensity or duration of the winds the confrontation would inspire. In this instance even the most pessimistic prediction would have been
an understatement.

Unlike the professionals on the fourteenth floor of the
courthouse, the lake-vessel crews would have shown scant interest in what was happening in faraway places such as Bismarck, North Dakota; Ely, Nevada; Amarillo, Texas; Trinidad, Colorado; Waynoka, Oklahoma; or Wichita, Kansas.
They took the weather as it came, and late on the afternoon
of November 10, slogging upbound on lower Lake Huron,
were the *Joseph H. Frantz* and Interlake Steamship Company's 420-foot *William B. Davock*, both with cargoes for
Lake Michigan ports. Off their starboard sides and on the
distant downbound course, either as smoke smudges during
daylight or flickering lights as darkness came on, were the
*Colonel, George F. Rand, Otto M. Reiss, Sir William Fair-
bairn, Fortwildoc* and *Thunder Bay Quarries*.

At noon on Monday, November 11, the *Davock* was only
ten minutes ahead of the *Henry Steinbrenner* as they were
reported passing Mackinaw City, in the Straits of Mackinac.
Nearly four hours later came the 320-foot *Anna C. Minch*,
followed shortly by the *Alberta* and *The Harvester*.

It started out as an unusually fine Monday morning on
Lake Michigan. Sundry vessels were going about their work-
a-day tasks with the unhurried, plodding pace that has forever
been the lot of steamboats. The *Ernest T. Weir* was threading
her way out of Green Bay at Porte Des Morts, heavy with ore
loaded at Escanaba. At Gary the *Governor Miller* was out-

bound, light, headed for Calcite and another stone cargo. The *Thomas F. Cole* and the *S. A. Robbins,* both light, left for Lake Superior ports. At South Chicago the *Harry W. Croft* and *J. A. Campbell* departed light with orders for Two Harbors while the *Novadoc* left with a cargo of powdered coke.

At Indiana Harbor the seven early-morning departures included the *Saturn* and *Frank Billings,* both light and upbound for stone, the *Saturn* to Port Inland, the *Billings* to Calcite. The other five were the loaded tankers *Justine C. Allen, Robert W. Stewart, Mercury, Maine* and the *New Haven Socony,* the latter scheduled for a relatively short voyage to Muskegon.

The *Frank J. Peterson* was in upper Lake Michigan after picking up scrap iron at Green Bay, and the *Sinaloa,* a self-unloading sand carrier, was about to depart after pumping sand in Little Bay de Noc.

Out of Milwaukee, after unloading coal cargoes, were the self-unloaders *Conneaut* and *Charles C. West.* The *Conneaut* was heading for the Straits of Mackinac, downbound to Lake Erie for another load of coal while the *Charles C. West* steamed south to fulfill another tonnage commitment at a lower Lake Michigan port.

At daybreak first assistant engineer John Schmitt of the *Charles C. West* was awakened by an insistent pounding on his door.

"What is it?" he asked, somewhat querulously.

"For gosh sakes," came the familiar voice of the porter. "Get your camera and come out here to see the prettiest sunrise you ever saw in your life."

Schmitt, a very capable movie enthusiast, dressed hurriedly

and went out on deck. "It was the most beautiful sight I have ever seen," he recalled. "The water reflected a thousand shades of red, orange and purple. It was like being caught in the middle of a giant rainbow and the sun just seemed to hang on the edge of the water like a painted backdrop."

The film Schmitt shot that morning was truly lovely, the kind one writes home about, although not as spectacular as the film he took the following morning, which was also the kind one writes home about, assuming that the photographer lived through it.

Propitiously, in view of what was to come, many vessels made their ports of destination about the same time others were committed to outbound cargoes or light voyages to various ports of call. At Escanaba the *Pathfinder* slid into an ore-loading berth soon after the *Ernest T. Weir* departed. At Indiana Harbor the scrap carrier *Tristan* prepared to depart for Muskegon while the tankers *Red Crown* and *William P. Cowan* tied up at the loading manifolds to gulp aboard thousands of gallons of oil and gasoline. The *Heron Bay* slipped in with a load of newsprint. At South Chicago the *James P. Walsh* hunkered under the coal-unloading buckets, while the *Lyman C. Smith* and *David P. Thompson* moored under the Huletts with ore from Two Harbors and Duluth. Nearby was the *John Sherwin* with ore from Ashland. Both the *J. S. Ashley* and *Harvey H. Brown* had arrived with limestone from Port Inland.

Unmindful of the heavy north-south traffic, the Ann Arbor, Grand Trunk and Pere Marquette carferries continued their cross-lake shuttle from Ludington, Grand Haven and Frankfort, Michigan, to Milwaukee and other Wisconsin cities. Busily at work, too, were a score or more sturdy fishing tugs, departing at daylight from a dozen Michigan and Wisconsin ports to lift distant nets. Among them were the *Dornbos, Richard H.* and *Indian*. They were tiny craft compared to the big steamers, but eminently seaworthy and skippered by experienced men. The *Dornbos* fished out of Charlevoix, and the *Indian* and *Richard H.* ghosted out between the South Haven piers at the first light of dawn.

At this point one wonders how many of the hundreds of sailors afloat on Lake Michigan that Monday morning recalled that in addition to being Armistice Day, it was exactly twenty-seven years ago to the day when the "Big Blow" of 1913 reached its murderous climax, sending eleven ships to the bottom with all hands and driving as many others ashore. Nearly three hundred seamen perished in that maelstrom spawned of a massive cyclonic storm of snow, unprecedented wind velocities, ice and thirty-five-foot seas. No, it was not a day to be easily forgotten, but if there were those of superstitious nature still sailing, they were not expressing their doubts or anxieties in sufficient numbers to inspire special prayer or supplication aboard ships or in shipping offices anywhere. Least of all was the United States Coast Guard cognizant of the fact that November had traditionally been the month of gales, storms and disaster on the Great Lakes. This was made very apparent when, in early October, with a full two months of shipping activity still ahead, the cutter *Escanaba,* a fast and sturdy rescue vessel, had been dry-docked for routine refitting!

The magnificent, rainbow-hued sunrise had presented a color spectrum of short duration. Shortly thereafter the sky grew gray and sullen and the mild southeast wind became fitfully brisk. At 9:15 A.M. the wind swung rapidly from southeast to southwest, and what had been happening in the tropopause and troposphere, with attending barometric pressure excesses in places like Bismarck, Ely, Amarillo, Trinidad, Waynoka and Wichita suddenly became very important to lake sailors, a matter of life and death, one might say.

The cyclone had developed in two separate cold fronts moving at a fantastically accelerated pace and only two hours apart as they swept generally from southwest to northeast from the prairie states, romping onward at thirty-five miles per hour. Heavy rains fell over the Mississippi Valley, followed by sleet, sixty-five-mile-per-hour winds and a temperature drop of forty-five degrees. Unseasonably heavy snows followed, from seventeen to twenty-three inches and ranging from western Iowa to central Minnesota. Thousands of motorists were stranded and hundreds of communities were isolated. In Iowa, Minnesota, Nebraska, South Dakota and Wisconsin thousands of cattle, sheep and hogs died in the fields. Orchards were decimated, farm buildings flattened and over 300,000 turkeys destined for the holiday market were wiped out. Towns and cities on the shores of Lake Michigan were assaulted by banshee winds that unroofed stores, homes and factories. Telephone and utility poles fell like dominoes and streets were littered with broken glass signs and tangles of wires.

The angling course of the storm first made its devastating impact known on the western end of Lake Superior. La Crosse, Wisconsin, recorded the lowest barometric pressure ever at that station. At Houghton, Michigan, and Duluth, Minnesota, the lowest readings of record were also registered. But in some cases the warnings put out at 6:30 A.M. by the U.S. Weather Bureau, when the storm was still centered over

Iowa, had already been heeded. At Duluth, where the *Edmund W. Mudge* was topping off her ore cargo, Captain W. Ross Maitland received orders from his Cleveland office to stay where he was until the storm was over. Other skippers, either on advice from owners or by taking a cue from Captain Maitland, put out more lines and stayed where they were, under the ore chutes.

But the warnings had come too late for some. Early that morning the *W. G. Pollock* had sailed with storage grain for Buffalo. But off the Apostle Islands her skipper changed his mind and hauled around to battle the seas all the way back to Duluth. Inbound and taking a frightful dusting from boarding seas that climbed right over her steering pole was the *Crescent City* with a deck load of automobiles taken on at Detroit. Captain Harold B. McCool knew he had to keep his vessel headed into the mountainous black seas, for to "fall off" into the troughs between them could be fatal. And keep her heading into them he did, although he witnessed a remarkable number of automobiles being swept overboard by the plundering graybeards.

"They just kept floating away like turtles," he later told a friend.

Other inbound vessels, once behind Minnesota Point, dropped their hooks in Duluth-Superior harbor and swung into the wind, like a flight of weather-bound ducks, automatically facing their adversary. With what any sympathetic sailor would term a sigh of relief the *Crescent City* joined a growing fleet already in the lee of the hills immediately behind the anchorage—the *Harry Coulby, N. F. Leopold, Merton E. Farr, Price McKinney, Sonora, Robert Fulton* and *Emory L. Ford.*

The unseasonably warm weather on Sunday and early Monday had inspired hundreds of duck hunters to celebrate the Armistice Day holiday at their favorite sport on inland lakes and the bottomlands of the Mississippi and Fox rivers. Unfortunately, they had dressed for the existing temperatures and were totally unprepared for the dramatic reversal of conditions. Fifty of them froze to death in their boats and blinds. Others were rescued more dead than alive.

Eleven o'clock on Monday morning was the designated time to observe a moment of silence and listen to appropriate tributes to our war dead in Chicago's Loop. It was not to be an extensive observance, just a few speeches and a showing of flags borne by World War I veterans. But even as the advance guard of Legionnaires began to gather at State and Madison streets, the oncoming storm, bulling along like a runaway locomotive, was already ending most emphatically a similar observance in Joliet, nearly forty miles to the southwest. The now-frigid wall of explosive wind, hail and shrapnel-like debris had scattered the sobered crowd in confusion. Store windows burst in, advertising signs were sent cartwheeling and utility poles and trees came thumping down.

Onward sped the storm, reaching the Loop in only fifteen minutes. Power lines were felled almost immediately, buried under hundreds of downed trees. Shingles burst from roofs like flocks of frightened birds. Chimneys collapsed to crash through homes and factories. A whisky manufacturer had spent almost $200,000 to erect a ten-story-high advertising sign at Randolph and the Outer Drive. In only a few minutes it twisted in the irresistible wind, sagged ominously and then folded up in a pile of mangled steel framework. Fearful of major structural damage, all lift and swing bridges over the

Calumet River were closed. Police and emergency switchboards were flooded with thousands of requests for assistance and reports of damage or dangerous conditions. In nearby Gary, Indiana, the top half of a 350-foot radio-transmitting tower folded up like a hairpin. Appropriately, its call letters were WIND!

So overpowering was the thrust and push of the storm that the water level of Lake Michigan at Chicago was lowered by almost five feet, causing the Calumet River to reverse its flow back into the lake. At Green Bay, to the north, a similar push of water to the east lowered the Fox River waters so drastically that a paper mill and a power plant were forced to suspend operations. This was the might, brawn and temper of the winds that thundered out over the length and breadth of Lake Michigan on Monday, November 11, 1940!

When Captain Robert W. Parsons took the *Thomas F. Cole* out between the breakwater pier lights at Gary shortly after four o'clock that morning, the weather was clear and the wind mild out of the southeast. But a forecast for possible high northeast winds puzzled him somewhat. Experience had proved that northeast gales are rarely spawned by southeast winds, but just as a precaution he set a course along the east shore of the lake to be in the lee of the land should the prediction prove correct. He could always haul out into deeper water should occasion demand. And this was substantially the thinking of Captain Harley O. Norton of the *New Haven Socony*. He was bound for Muskegon, on the east shore anyway. The midnight forecast had indeed warned of a possible northeasterly swing of the wind to gale proportions, but the 6:00 A.M. version had placed a storm center over Iowa, approaching rapidly and now generating southwesterly winds of gale stature. But he, too, should conditions necessitate, could haul his vessel around and steer a course over deeper water. Two hours ahead of the *New Haven Socony* was the 253-foot canaler *Novadoc,* South Chicago to Fort William with powdered coke. Like his counterparts on the *Thomas F. Cole* and *New Haven Socony,* Captain Donald Steip had chosen the "short route" up the east coast of the lake, but much closer to shore.

Downbound on the same east-shore course, after clearing Grays Reef and steering 217 degrees, SW ¾ S, the Manitou Passage course, were the *William B. Davock* and the *Anna C. Minch,* two of the vessels reported as transiting the Straits of Mackinac as of noon and early afternoon. The *Davock* was loaded with coal for South Chicago, the *Minch,* with grain screenings from Fort William, destined for Chicago. At the time, the *Minch* was thought to be the only bulk freighter on the lakes bearing the name of a woman. The *Davock* was heard clearly on the radio-telephone, Captain Charles W. Allen pinpointing his position and commenting that the weather was unusually mild, despite the lateness of the season.

Considering that every vessel and its people comprise literally a small and compact village, each of its inhabitants having his own abstruse goals, motivations, problems and personal considerations, the *Davock* could probably be termed rather typical of the times. With a crew of thirty-two she had steamed out of Erie, Pennsylvania, without the services of oiler Durward S. Farr. The twenty-four-year-old Farr, with only a couple of more trips scheduled, had quit, thereby sacrificing his seasonal bonus. But young Farr was in love with Marcella Jenness, back in Ashtabula, Ohio, and by his own admission "had a bellyful of steamboating for one year." Miss Jenness, as it transpired, was mildly annoyed at his relinquishing the bonus which had figured prominently in their marriage plans. His good friend aboard the *Davock* was a nineteen-year-old porter, Charles Flint, whose father worked with Farr's father on the Pennsylvania Railroad's ore dock at Ashtabula. Buddies, too, in the *Davock*'s fo'c'sle were deckhands James Saunders and Sterling Wood, both nineteen. It was Wood's first job, his shipboard earnings budgeted to augment a $200 scholarship he had received from Baldwin-Wallace College. Young Saunders was the son of Captain T. Howard Saunders, skipper of the *Jay C. Morse,* also of the Interlake Steamship fleet. The *Morse,* at the time the *Davock* headed down Lake Michigan, was on Lake Erie, enroute to Toledo for coal after unloading ore at Buffalo. Rejoining the *Davock* from the mail boat at Detroit was oiler Charles Findlay, also from Ashtabula and one of six men from that city aboard. He had taken a few days off to have an injured hand treated. These comings and goings were all part of steamboating and an accepted part of shipboard life.

On the Canadian vessel *Anna C. Minch,* less than four hours' steaming time astern of the *Davock,* the crew undoubtedly had similar personnel changes. It is significant to note that in addition to Captain Donald A. Kennedy, five other crewmen were from the same city, Collingwood, Ontario, and seven were from nearby Midland or the immediate area. It was part of an old Great Lakes tradition, particularly in Canada, of hiring qualified friends, neighbors or fellow townsmen, especially when jobs were few and far between. It was fine when all went well, but utter disaster to the communities when tragedy struck.

Leaving behind a woeful trail of snowy desolation and un-paralladed damage ashore, the storm roared on with undiminished speed, encompassing all of Lake Michigan.

It was the custom of many shipmasters, rather proud of their own prognosticating abilities, developed through years of experience, to take the official weather predictions with a grain of salt, perhaps several. Others tempered their own observations with official opinion, often finding that both sources were subject to considerable leeway. But there was no mistaking the extremely low-hanging bank of darkness that moved out from the land all the way from Buffington Harbor to Manistique, a sinister panorama of frazzled gray clouds of varying hues, obviously in torment and rolling on-ward in disarray, like battalions of undisciplined soldiers, sacking and pillaging in unbridled fury. Below the raggedy formations appeared to be a confused and dark curtain that could have been rain, hail or simply surface water picked up and borne onward by the furious winds. This was it!

Captain Norton of the *New Haven Socony* knew exactly what was coming, and immediately hauled around to port, heading his vessel into the wind and away from the lee shore. Captain Parsons of the *Thomas F. Cole* did precisely the same thing in seeking deeper waters, away from the clutching sands near the east shore. Ahead of them, still pounding up the lake, Captain Steip of the *Novadoc* would have undoubt-edly preferred to follow suit. But the wind had come on so suddenly and the seas had risen so ominously that he was powerless to swing his vessel's head around into the storm. He was between Muskegon and Little Sable Point, only a scant few hundred yards offshore, and there was nothing he could do about it but plug ahead and hope for the best. He tried many times to bring her around but failed. The *Nova-doc,* though relatively small, was adequately powered, and her failure to respond was puzzling. Later, Captain Steip was to confide to his friend and neighbor, Captain Wilf Lemcke, that either the firemen were seasick or the quality of his coal bunkers was so poor that adequate steam pressure could not be maintained.

With dusk came snow, heavy flurries driven in horizontal sheets by the wind, still increasing in velocity and wreaking havoc in communities along the east shore. Gusts of up to one hundred miles per hour lifted roofs from factories, blew down chimneys and flattened utility poles and trees by the thousands. At Ludington, Michigan, Captain A. E. Christoffersen, in charge of the Coast Guard station, ordered the tower watchman down from his post at 11:00 P.M. fearing that the structure would collapse. In any event, visibility from the tower was nil, and having a man stationed there was an exercise in futility. At almost the same moment two big carferries had come to grief almost within hailing distance of the station. *No. 21,* in attempting to dock, made the harbor with difficulty but was driven against old pilings. Worse yet, the flagship of the Pere Marquette fleet, the *City of Flint,* missed the entrance piers, the wind and seas carrying her broadside to and on the beach north of the breakwater. Assaulted by thirty-foot seas, she was in grave danger until her skipper ordered the sea cocks opened, allowing her to settle firmly in the sand to prevent the hull from pounding. The cry of "shipwreck" brought hundreds of spectators to the beach as searchlights were played upon the scene. The crowd was awed by the sight of big seas exploding over the *City of Flint's* starboard flank, flinging spray and spume as

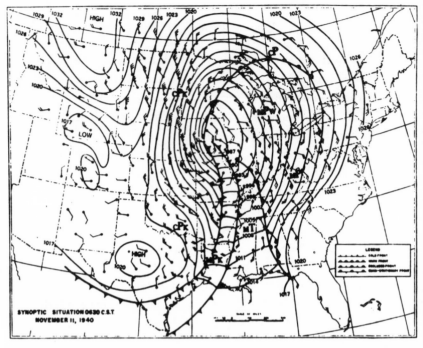

SYNOPTIC SITUATION 0630 C.S.T.
NOVEMBER 11, 1940

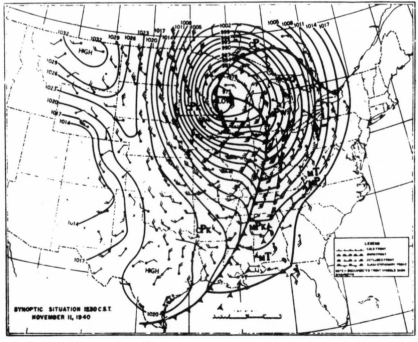

SYNOPTIC SITUATION 1230 C.S.T.
NOVEMBER 11, 1940

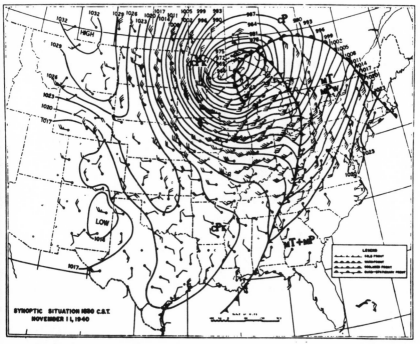

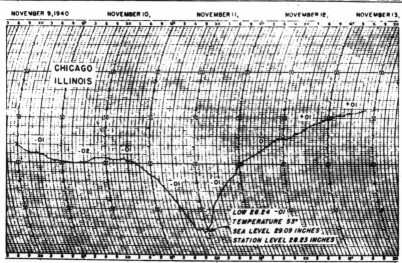

SWIRLING LINES ON UNITED STATES WEATHER BUREAU SYNOPTIC
SITUATION MAPS ILLUSTRATE THE LOW PRESSURE FRONTS OF THE
ARMISTICE DAY STORM DEVELOPING AND INTENSIFYING OVER THE
UPPER MIDWEST. *Lower right:* BAROGRAPH CHART DEPICTS THE OM-
INOUS LOW PRESSURE PREVAILING ON NOVEMBER 11, 1940.

high as her masthead. But with heat and light, she was in no immediate danger and the crew of forty-eight and four passengers remained aboard. But at that moment, of course, they had little choice.

South of Ludington the beleaguered *Novadoc* was still slogging along perilously close to the beach, battered by wind and seas. Poor Captain Steip knew that his vessel was being driven closer to the clutching breakers every moment, and that, inevitably, she would go aground. He advised his crew of this certainty and instructed them to stay wherever they were and under no circumstances to venture out on deck. He had set his course far too close to shore, knew it, and now could do nothing but wait for the moment of truth and retribution.

From the lighthouse tower at Little Sable Point, keeper William Krewell spotted the *Novadoc*'s masthead lights swinging in awesome arches as she rolled outrageously in the confused seas caused by incoming graybeards meeting the backwash from the beach. He knew not which vessel she was but realized that she was in immediate and mortal peril. Stinging sheets of snow and sleet blotted her from view for long periods, but in one brief instant of improved visibility he saw her lights blink out suddenly and knew that she had stranded. While Krewell rushed to notify the Ludington Coast Guard station, the assistant keeper, Henry Vavrina, grabbed his flashlight and ran to the beach to signal to the stricken *Novadoc* that her plight had been noted. Half frozen, he repeated his signals for what seemed to him a long time but got no response.

Meanwhile, as the night wore on, the *William B. Davock* and *Anna C. Minch,* long since committed to the downbound east-shore route, steered 217 degrees on a course that would take them sixty-five miles between the mainland and the Beaver and Fox islands to Manitou Passage. There, a course alteration to 244 degrees, maintained for fourteen miles, would take them safely between South Manitou Island and Sleeping Bear Point. Then another change of course to 214 degrees for nineteen miles would put them off Point Betsie where the final courses for lower Lake Michigan ports would be set. It was the usual route for average draft vessels and approximately fifty miles shorter than the other choice of steering westward from the Straits of Mackinac past White Shoal and Lansing Shoal lights before hauling around to port off Seul Choix Point and heading down the lake. It was not the course skippers would have chosen had they been aware of the monstrous storm they might encounter. There was just not that much maneuvering room for a vessel sore beset by the cylonic witches' brew of wind, sea, snow and ice that fell upon Lake Michigan late on that grim Monday. It was Armistice Day ashore, but for a score of vessels fighting for their lives, there was no peace out on the lake that night.

Daybreak brought no respite from the storm. The seas were now revealed in all their frightening immensity. The *City of Flint,* with passengers and crew still aboard, was being pounded by wind and wave. The *Novadoc,* in the morning light, was just where lightkeeper Krewell said she would be, 150 yards offshore, half submerged and with her back broken. Peering through the snow and blowing sand, those on shore were in doubt as to whether there was life aboard the vessel, hidden in the lather of each sea that climbed vengefully over her. Yet, on occasions watchers were sure they could see life and movement in the pilot house.

Few sailors, even those who had weathered the "Big Blow" of 1913, could recall seas that built up so quickly to such frightening heights. They rolled on in relentless assaults, dark, menacing and thirty-five feet from troughs to crests. By noon on Tuesday, the twelfth, movie-buff engineer John Schmitt, the man who had photographed the magnificent sunrise on Monday, was huddled in the lee of the *Charles C. West*'s Texas deck, capturing on film some of the most dramatic storm footage ever recorded, massive dark seas that reared up as high as the top of the *West*'s funnel.

Time-wise, the first victim of the storm was thought to be the *Sinaloa* as the initial impact centered on the island and shoal-studded upper sector of the lake. While in Green Bay and nearing Porte Des Morts (Death's Door in Great Lakes terminology), she got caught in tremendous cross seas, rolling so violently that her steam lines broke at dusk on Monday, leaving her powerless and without steering capability. During the wild night she drifted with the wind, still rolling wickedly, until she grounded on a reef off Sac Bay, near the tip of Garden Peninsula, in Big Bay de Noc. The after end crew fastened a line to a buoy. When it drifted ashore, the line was attached by fishermen to a small boat which the crew drew back to the vessel. Then, in repeated trips, although the little craft swamped several times, the sailors reached shore. Some had to make it by going hand over hand the last hundred yards. Two of them, oiler Jack LeCost and his father, a fireman, concluding that their steamboating was over for the season, walked up the beach to their farm home!

The *Frank J. Peterson,* a World War I three-island steamer engaged in carrying package freight, scrap and new automobiles, got caught at the western approaches to the Straits of

Mackinac. She tried to turn but was driven hard ashore on St. Helena Island. Not far away the 415-foot *Conneaut* was ashore at Epoufette, near Pelkie Reef, her bottom heavily damaged, the rudder torn away and her propeller stripped. Her crew, the captain reported over the radio-telephone, wanted to be removed as soon as possible. Surrounded by shoals and rocks near Gray's Reef, the *Frank Billings* was reported asking for assistance after windows in her pilot house had been shattered, her helmsman injured and some of her forward quarters flooded. Her skipper, Captain Harold Murphy, later denied asking for help. Far to the south, off South Haven, the tanker *Justine C. Allen,* outbound from Indiana Harbor, radioed that she had broken a rudder cable in monstrous seas and was in danger of going aground although frantic efforts to repair the cable were under way. Coast Guardsmen and volunteers set up a beach watch for her. Unreported and feared lost were the tankers *Mercury* and *Crudoil.* Also far overdue and believed lost were the South Haven fishing tugs *Richard H.* and *Indian.* Frantic families of those aboard watched as four daring Coast Guardsmen, under boatswain's mate Elmer Dudley, put out into the towering seas in a thirty-six-foot surfboat to search for the missing boats and men. Before departing the dock Dudley topped off his fuel load at two hundred gallons.

Ashore, where land line communications had been disrupted in many areas, the Lorain County Radio Corporation, pioneers in ship-to-shore radio-telephone systems, was experiencing its busiest day ever. Five operators were "on the horn" at the Lorain station and additional operators were also called in at the firm's Duluth and Port Washington stations. Most of the messages were between ship captains and ship owners and were handled on four channels instead of the usual two. Distress messages were instantly relayed to the Coast Guard.

South of Grand Haven, beach watchers found evidence of tragedy. From the surf and on the sands they retrieved the top of a pilot house, doors, oars and parts of a shattered life-boat, distinctly lettered *New Haven Socony*. Had Captain Harley O. Norton, despite his quick haul to port to get his vessel headed into the blow, gone down with his ship and men? All the items in the welter of wreckage seemed to indicate just such a dreadful fate. And who knew, ere the day was over, what other relics of disaster might come in on the towering breakers still roaring in from the lake.

As a matter of fact, the *New Haven Socony* did come very close to vanishing in the overwhelming seas. Tankers generally present a low profile and she was no exception. The seas swept away her lifeboats, ventilators, stanchions and deck gear. A succession of ugly crests subsequently cleaned her pilot house of furniture, compass and charts. Then one monster took away the pilot house itself, leaving Captain Norton and his helmsman standing there by the wheel stand, drenched with each boarding sea. Ice continued to pile up on the little tanker, and when she finally made port at Chicago she looked more like an iceberg than a vessel, her freeboard reduced to only eighteen inches by the sheer weight of ice.

The deep-water course Captain Parsons elected for the *Thomas F. Cole* when he noted the approach of the storm took him well away from the lee shore, but put his vessel nose to nose with the worst seas he could recall. They climbed up over the bow, rolled ten feet high over the spar deck and thundered against the after cabins. The telephone system was disrupted and a companionway door to the engine room was torn away. Most of the after cabin plating was crushed in, allowing the incoming seas to ravish the accommodations before pouring down into the engine room. The steward's big cookstove broke loose, charging about like a mad monster, demolishing the other fixtures and grinding the paneling to splinters. Then the stove itself disintegrated and the whole pile of wreckage, dishes, pans, food, wood and utensils slid wildly from side to side as the ship rolled to a terrifying degree with each sea.

These conditions prevailed until late Monday night when the wind and sea backed down, and Captain Parsons could make a survey of his vessel. The damage aft he was aware of, what concerned him was the condition of the hull itself, alternately hogging, sagging and twisting in the wrenching seas. What he found below, in the empty cargo holds, was dismaying evidence of near disaster. Long rows of rivets had been sheared off, the weakened plates grinding and creaking ominously. Quickly ordering the *Cole*'s speed reduced to half-speed to minimize vibration, he steered a cautious course to Milwaukee. It had taken the *Cole* fifty hours to steam one hundred miles on a voyage that ended in a shipyard for extensive repairs and refitting.

Into several ports crept battered steamers, lucky survivors of the worst Lake Michigan storm in many years. The tanker *Crudoil,* listed as missing and believed lost, limped into Sturgeon Bay with six feet of water in her holds, and her topsides cleaned of boats, raft and deck gear. Also thought lost was the tanker *Mercury,* but she finally made port after "riding it out" in shelter behind North Manitou Island. The

*Empire State,* after losing her rudder and going aground, reached safety at Green Bay.

Another near victim was the *W. H. McGean,* so savagely mauled by the seas that her crew had several times resigned themselves to going down with their ship. Seas crashed against the bow with such force that bunks and furniture were torn loose to toss around like jackstraws. Officers were unable to reach the pilot house to relieve the captain and wheelmen, who stood alone in the wind and water that crashed through the pilot-house windows for thirty-two hours. Aft the seas plucked away the ventilators and skylight, pounded through bulkheads and ravished the galley. The engine room and fire hole were flooded. Crewmen reported seas so high that they went right over the smoke stack. Into Chicago came the *Joseph Block* with her pilot house damaged and her crew's quarters cleaned out. The *Henry Steinbrenner* tied up for extensive repairs and *The Harvester* was so badly damaged that she went immediately into drydock. On Lake Superior the *Sparta* was aground and totally wrecked near Munising.

While some shipowners were happily receiving word that their vessels were safe, and others were assessing their losses, a bitter controversy was raging in Ludington. It was a known fact the *Novadoc* had gone aground off Juniper Beach on Monday evening, that there was still life aboard, and as of late Tuesday the Ludington Coast Guard station had made no attempt at rescue. Sarcastic inquiries got only the gruff response that Captain Christoffersen was of the opinion that shooting a line out to the stranded vessel would only endanger those aboard who would have to expose themselves on deck to secure it. To many this was a completely unsatisfactory explanation. In the opinion of most experienced sailors, of which Ludington had an ample supply, the Coast Guard was derelict to duty in allowing the *Novadoc*'s crew to freeze to death while the service had supposedly unsinkable surf-boats and adequate beach gear to effect a rescue by breeches buoy. It was also a fact that, even after outspoken critics had made their point, Captain Christoffersen permitted the situation to remain status quo for still another full night.

On Wednesday morning, when the seas had quieted somewhat, the Coast Guard belatedly prepared a rescue boat. But they were too late. As if it were a routine assignment, Captain Clyde Cross of the fishing tug *Three Brothers,* along with his crew of Gustave Fisher and Joe Fountain, chugged out to take off the seventeen *Novadoc* men who had waited desperately for rescue throughout thirty-six hellish hours. They had been separated, most of the crew huddled in the pilot house, the after crew seeking refuge in the galley.

When the *Novadoc* had first gone aground on Monday night Captain Steip had sent up flares, but these could not be seen due to heavy snow. On Tuesday morning, when the hull had sagged suddenly, cook Joe Shane and his helper, Philip Flavin, became panic-stricken and made a wild dash forward over the broken deck. Fireman John Peterson, peering through a porthole, saw Shane clinging to a railing and seconds later witnessed a sea that took both the cook and railing overboard. He also saw Flavin disappear after apparently being struck by wreckage.

All through the day on Tuesday the *Novadoc*'s crew, without heat or food, scanned the shoreline for some evidence of rescue equipment being mobilized. But beyond the helpless spectators huddled around bonfires there was no sign of a

Coast Guard boat, portable beach equipment, line-throwing gun or a breeches buoy tripod. Darkness came again and the hopeless men could do little but try to survive another night.

The fiasco of a Coast Guard station and its command officer unwilling to perform the basic function for which the service existed was completely contrary to the otherwise sparkling image of heroics with which it had been traditionally associated. In Ludington, where the economy of the community was largely dependent upon the operations of the Pere Marquette carferry fleet, feelings were running high. The plea that much of the station's personnel was tied up in assisting the *City of Flint* did not allay the honest anger of knowledgeable sailors. The carferry was practically on the beach, and had heat and light; her people were in no real or immediate danger. Out on the *Novadoc*, however, a crew was freezing and starving. Unflattering comparisons with the legendary bravery of the old U.S. Lifesaving Service were made.

But what stature the Coast Guard lost at Ludington was, in a measure, compensated for at South Haven where daring boatswain's mate Elmer Dudley had taken out the station's thirty-six-foot surfboat to search for the fishing tugs *Richard H.* and *Indian*. The surfboat had soon disappeared in the valleys between the seas, and there were some observers who concluded on the spot that Dudley and his men would inevitably be lost. But, almost incredibly, the next day the boat and crew chugged into port on the far side of the lake, heavily burdened with ice and with only twenty gallons of fuel left. However gallant, their search was obviously fruitless even before it began. The little surfboat had scarcely been lost from sight when word came that wreckage of both the

*Richard H.* and *Indian* had been found on the beach south of their home port.

But what of the *William B. Davock* and *Anna C. Minch,* the pair of vessels that had set their angling courses down the east coast of Lake Michigan after transiting the Straits of Mackinac and rounding Gray's Reef? They were still unreported. Although experienced marine men know that radio-telephone aerials are frequently among the casualties in a really stiff blow, there should have been word or a sighting by now.

In the Cleveland office of the Interlake Steamship Company, the first inkling of disaster was a telephone message from an Associated Press reporter, advising marine superintendent Captain Thomas E. Zealand that the *Davock* had apparently foundered; bodies were even then coming ashore in the vicinity of Ludington.

After confirming the report with the Ludington Coast Guard station, Captain Zealand immediately delegated a team of three men to depart posthaste to help in the recovery and identification of the victims and to assist in any way possible. He nominated Roy Meyer, in charge of vessel personnel, to head the group which included William Eckert and veteran engineer George Manthey. They left Cleveland by train, in less than two hours after word of the tragedy had been received.

Now, too, with the radio-telephone channels busy with messages, the fate of *Davock,* and probably the *Minch,* was quickly known all over the lakes. On the *Jay C. Morse* a grief-stricken Captain T. Howard Saunders could do little but recall happier times with his son James, a *Davock* deckhand. On another Interlake vessel mate George Hanson [1] remembered his good friend Jere Collins, the *Davock*'s first assistant engineer, and the day when fate blessed them both with advancement in the ranks. Both had been enjoying a beer at an Ashtabula Harbor tavern while their vessel, the *Fayette Brown*, was being unloaded. Hanson was a wheelsman, Collins an oiler. Their skipper sought them out to inpart the glad tidings. The company, due to increased business, had activated another vessel, thus providing a step-up in rank for the pair, Hanson to third mate, Collins to third engineer. This news, obviously called for another round.

Bad news, as they say, travels fast, and in six homes back in Ashtabula the tidings brought tears and a mustering of family solace. But in two other homes, those of ex-oiler Durward S. Farr and his fiancée, Marcella Jenness, there was the stunned realization that fate had miraculously saved them. Now, somehow, that end-of-the-season bonus didn't seem very important.

The men of the *Davock* and *Minch* were not long in finding their way ashore, sodden burdens that rolled restlessly in the surf or lay quietly in the sand. From a point a mile or two above Pentwater to the beach north of Ludington they wandered in amidst a clutter of life rings, broken lifeboats, oars, cabin doors, fragments of furniture and a fluffy mixture of grain screenings from the *Minch*—young deckhands James Saunders and his buddy, Sterling Wood; second mate John Wiesen; first mate Charles Price; wheelsmen Andy Stiffler and Walter Kiewice; and watchmen James Bowman, Lawrence Bleshoy and Martin Chambers. With the common trait of sailors to seek the company of friends, they were joined there by others—oiler George Sovey, second engineer James Becker, deckhand Lawrence Thompson and first mate

Richard Elyea, all from the *Minch.* Slowly, as time went on, they continued their reluctant rendezvous with land, the veterans and the beginners, all treated as equals by the cruel seas.

Roy Meyer and his associates, upon arriving in Ludington early Wednesday morning, went immediately to the Dorrell Funeral Home and then across the street to the Salvation Army Home where the recovered bodies lay in neat rows. Meyer was armed with what was a depressing but useful document compiled at the start of the season, a listing of the ages, heights, weights and known physical peculiarities of the *Davock's* crewmen: Joseph Rakowski, two scars on chest; James Gordon, tattoo on each forearm; Carl Sharrow, scar on left side of head, birthmark on right shoulder; Charles Findley, recent injury to right hand; Lyle Doyle, three fingers off left hand; Charles Ferguson, tattoo mark on each shoulder; Orville Shurkey, burn scar on left forearm; Homer Younkins, scar on right leg, below knee; and Harold Mullen, scar from thyroid operation.

Of the eleven *Davock* crewmen thus far recovered when the men from Cleveland arrived, eight had already been identified. In one instance there was an obvious error, brought about because the body of young Sterling Wood had been clothed in a jacket that contained the discharge book of wheelsman Andy Stiffler. This left the other without a name, and yet the features were familiar. Meyer had a photograph of a man with similar facial characteristics and when he drew a mustache on it the identification was made. Andy Stiffler had grown his mustache after the photograph had been taken!

Meyer, too, found Captain Christoffersen, the Ludington Coast Guard officer, singularly uncooperative. Once, when he called after learning that one of the station's crew might have some helpful information, he was told that the man in question was repairing an aerial and couldn't be disturbed, and that he, Christoffersen, was too busy to talk. On another occasion Meyer visited the station to consult a lake chart. Christoffersen merely pointed in the direction of the chart table, not bothering to rise from his seat to be of assistance. And once again when Meyer called the station he was told that the Captain was "on leave."

In combing the beaches the three Clevelanders found that unthinking souvenir hunters had already carted away much debris that could possibly have been of help, and that the shoreline was still littered with wreckage. Walking for miles, they found both of the *Davock*'s lifeboats, one damaged, the other intact but full of water. Tarpaulins, part of what had once been an ice box, a section of the captain's desk and other debris, much of it unidentifiable, was strewn for miles. Along the beach they met Captain Scott Misener, president of Sarnia Steamships Ltd., operators of the *Anna C. Minch*. He, too, was seeking the rest of his twenty-four people and wreckage he could identify with his vessel.

North of Ludington, Meyer spotted a familiar object, a large wicker chair. More importantly, he knew exactly where it had come from.

"I had been aboard the *Davock* a few weeks earlier," recalled Meyer. "In Captain Allen's office I noticed this big wicker chair and commented that it looked wider than the door through which it would have had to be carried to get it in the office. Captain Allen said that this was true, but that while wicker was quite pliable they had done considerable twisting and bending to get it in. I knew then, when I saw that same chair on the beach, that the forward cabins had come off the *Davock* when she went down."

Bearing out this theory was the fact that up until that point all the bodies recovered were those of crewmen normally housed in the forward quarters—deck officers, wheelsmen, deckhands and watchmen. Lawrence Gonyea, the *Davock*'s steward, did not make his way ashore until the following Sunday, November 17, the first member of the after-end crew to be found. Fireman Frank Parker didn't make it until the thirtieth. Another tardy wanderer found the beach on December 18, but bore none of the identifying scars, moles, tattoos or dental peculiarities noted on Meyer's list. The only clue, and it subsequently proved to be unrewarding, was a gold signet ring bearing initials that appeared to be "T.F." and an inscription inside, "From Mother."

Two more seamen made a belated appearance north of Ludington later in the month. One was a Canadian, a late arrival from the Minch. The other could not be identified.

When further intensified attempts at identification of the two strangers, now in Mr. Dorrell's establishment, failed, the Interlake Steamship Company authorized the purchase of a plot in Ludington's Lakeview Cemetery. There, in suitable caskets and with floral offerings and simple services they were laid to rest, two more sailors who, like others in similar plots along the Great Lakes, are "known but to God."

Four days after the storm Clyde Cross, hero of the *Novadoc* rescue, took his tug *Three Brothers* out to scout around. After three hours of searching he was heading home when, a little over a mile south of Pentwater and not far from shore, he saw something protruding from the water. At first he thought it was a sea gull, but as the tug drew near he found it to be the very tip of a mast or spar. The object that had reminded him of a sea gull was a swinging metal wind-direction pennant.[2] It was immediately identified by Sarnia Steamships people as being from the *Minch*. Below the spar Cross thought he could see the outlines of a pilot house.

A later examination of the sunken vessel by divers revealed that 120 feet of her after end was missing. This immediately conjured up the picture of the *Minch* and *Davock*, fighting desperately in the gale of wind and blinding snow and frantically trying to keep out of the troughs of the seas, colliding in a fearful embrace that left no survivors. Other searchers, by plane and boat, vainly sought the grave of the *Davock*.

Although the collision theory was largely accepted as fact by many sailors, it has recently been discounted by the discovery in May, 1972, of the *Davock*'s hull, upside down in 204 feet of water off Little Sable Point. Working from a former fishing tug equipped with sonar and other sophisticated gear, divers Kent Bellrichard, John Steele and William Cohrs explored the hulk briefly, but could find no evidence of a collision. The obvious conclusion then, is that both vessels foundered from simple stress of weather, their proximity to each other merely coincidental. It is easy to visualize the *Minch*, with Captain Donald Kennedy striving mightily to keep his vessel out of the troughs, with her bow uplifted by a giant sea, her after end rising on the crest of another. Then she probably just broke in two as her unsupported, grain-laden midbody sagged fatally. The divers found the *Davock*'s rudder cramped hard to port, as though she, too, were trying to fight her way out of a valley between monstrous seas. Here again her final moments were predictable, an overwhelming sea, or a series of them, rolling her over and sending her down.

Sailors and landsmen alike have long argued over which was the worst of the great November storms since the turn of the century, the "Big Blow" of 1913 or the Armistice Day maelstrom of 1940. Both were cyclonic in nature, both had about the same intensity of wind speed and the same ice-producing plummeting of temperatures. Those who hold that the Armistice Day storm was equal in destructive forces point out that only the ship-to-shore radio-telephone, better dissemination of weather information and automatic direction finders kept down the toll of vessels. Others maintain that the 1913 storm, with eleven big boats lost with all hands, was by far the worst of the two, largely because it covered a greater geographic area.

But in at least two of several such burial plots along the shores of the Great Lakes—Goderich, Ontario, where nameless victims of the 1913 storm lie, and in Ludington's Lakeview Cemetery—the question would be moot, particularly to the man who wore a token of a woman's devotion, a signet ring "From Mother."

¹ George Hanson, the ex-wheelsman who recalled his friend Jere Collins, the lost *Davock's* first assistant engineer, rose through the ranks to become skipper of several Interlake Steamship Company vessels, eventually commanding the fleet's flagship, the *John Sherwin.*

² The *Minch's* metal wind pennant, plucked from the sunken vessel's forward spar by Clyde Cross, was later presented to Stan Kennedy, of Port Colborne, Ontario, brother of Captain Donald A. Kennedy who went down with his ship. Stan Kennedy later gave the pennant, with a suitable inscription plate, to the Huron Institute, at Collingwood, Ontario. Six of the *Minch's* crew were from Collingwood.

# 6

~~~~~~~~~
~~~~~~~
~~~

# *The Wandering "Ghost"*
## *of the Great Lakes*

T<sub>HE</sub> *Jupiter,* if size alone is a criteria, wasn't much even for her time, which was roughly seventy-odd years ago. Although she had a life span of over half a century, it took her forty-six years to make big news. Even this was a dozen years after shrinking earnings had encouraged her owners, the Interlake Steamship Company, to sell her, in the spring of 1936. The Interlake people, operators of a vast fleet, were, over the years, fond of naming their boats after planets or stars of varying magnitudes in the heavenly constellations, as if beseeching celestial blessings for vessels built by mortal man. As witness, in addition to the *Jupiter,* came the *Canopus, Arcturus, Perseus, Sirius, Taurus, Uranus, Vega, Venus, Cepheus, Cetus, Corvus, Cygnus, Indus, Lupus, Mars, Neptune, Pegasus, Regulus* and *Saturn.* It was almost as though all the firm's partners and stockholders were dedicated amateur astronomers and inveterate star gazers, each with his favorite. The *Jupiter,* thirty-five years old and small, was expendable.

Although the 346-foot steamer had ceased to pay her own

way in the iron ore and coal trade, her new owners, the Great Lakes Silica Company, concluded that she was ideal for the sand, stone, scrap and pig-iron trade. However, the best-laid plans of mice and businessmen often go awry, which was exactly the case with the *Jupiter*. Lack of anticipated cargoes and extensive and expensive conversions and repairs resulted in the vessel being moored at her dock most of the time, which was precisely where she was when lawyers for the American Hoist & Derrick Company, the Crane Company and a considerable array of other clients libeled her. The claims, shrewd and knowledgeable marine men said, would total well over $50,000. Legal machinations, after her owners filed for bankruptcy, took most of the winter, but in April of 1937, the United States Marshal's office, acting on order of Federal Court, put the old *Jupiter* up for sale at public auction, affixing a minimum bid of $75,000. Strangely enough, after surveyors for several prospective bidders roamed over and through her hull and quarters, tapping rivets and inspecting her boilers, not a single bid was forthcoming.

A month later Marshal George J. Keniath announced that the *Jupiter* had been sold to Blake Womer for $70,000. It was obvious that the ship's creditors had since concluded that part of a loaf was better than none, the price being sufficient to pay them off at about eighty cents on the dollar.

The Womer acquisition then soon evolved into the Jupiter Steamship Company with the astute Walter C. Secord named manager. Now Mr. Secord, unlike the previous extremely short-term management, was a sharp, canny operator with good connections all over the lakes. Only those in this almost fraternal-like industry can appreciate the significance of this experience, know-how and entrée into the charmed circles where cargoes are chartered and tonnage commitments made.

The *Jupiter* came alive almost at once, Mr. Secord somehow managing to scrounge up cargoes of salt, pig iron, wire coils, scrap and grain. Her limited capacity of 5600 gross tons and formidable operating costs ruled her out of the long-haul iron-ore trade, but she was eminently qualified for the other, relatively short-haul commodities. When she was activated for the 1939 season her master was the popular Captain Fred W. Thodey of Port Huron, Michigan, first grand vice-president of the International Shipmasters' Association, and her chief engineer, Herbert Muhlitner of St. Clair, Michigan.

Great Lakes vessels, because they are not subject to the corrosive influence of saltwater, outlast their deep-sea sisters by decades. So, despite the fact that the *Jupiter* was in her thirty-ninth year, it was decided, in 1940, that her performance would benefit by the installation of a new, streamlined rudder. This was done quickly and efficiently in mid-summer at the Toledo Ship Building Company.

The war in Europe had so greatly intensified the demand for bulk raw materials at Great Lakes ports that the 1940 season was a protracted one. Luckily, the *Jupiter* was elsewhere when the great Armistice Day storm of November 11 hit Lake Michigan, so she was able to plug along with whatever cargoes Mr. Secord had secured for her. On December 11, on her last trip of the long season, the *Jupiter* stood just inside Saginaw Bay, on lower Lake Huron, with a cargo of pig iron destined for a foundry in Saginaw, where, incidentally, she was to lay up. But winter had come early and most of the bay was covered with a five-inch layer of hard blue ice. After a couple of tentative thrusts and firm rebuffs, her master, doubtless mindful of her age and indicated horse-power of only 1480, withdrew to the edge of the ice field and called for assistance. The Coast Guard Cutter *Tahoma,* only recently transferred from Cleveland to Sault Ste. Marie, had scarcely settled down at her new moorings when she was ordered to depart immediately to break a channel through the bay ice and into the Saginaw River and the foundry dock. When this most difficult task was accomplished and the heavy winter mooring lines secured, the crew, and one must assume the *Jupiter,* too, heaved a long sigh of relief.

The *Jupiter* opened the 1941 Saginaw Bay season by steaming through the ten-mile field of deteriorated ice on April 12, bound for Duluth and a grain cargo the energetic Mr. Secord had made available. But she had a new skipper now, Captain Thomas Greenway, and good old Herb Muhlitner was still giving her engine tender loving care. Both were to be involved in the trying times that lay ahead.

Beyond the peak demands for iron ore and grain to supply the nations under siege of Nazi forces on land and sea, and after Pearl Harbor our own military and industrial complex, the 1940s were to be tumultuous years on the lakes. The C.I.O.–National Maritime Union was striving desperately to organize the shipping fleets and the *Jupiter* quickly became a pawn. Logically the N.M.U. sought first to pick off and consolidate their gains in the smaller fleets, and the little Jupiter Steamship Company was one of the first targets.

Troubles for the *Jupiter* came first at Duluth on the second day of August when four officers and eight seamen, all union members, left the ship at the Northwestern Coal Dock. Short-handed, so much so that he was denied permission to sail, Captain Greenway backed into the harbor basin and dropped anchor to await replacements. There, five days later, she was being picketed in a most unusual manner—union representatives circling her in rowboats and carrying signs decrying the owner's unwillingness to negotiate or bargain. Eventually a shipboard election was held and the union lost. Once more the *Jupiter* went about her business.

But the union people, having lost but one battle, continued the war—charges, countercharges, hearings and elections, highlighting waterfront and shipboard conversations for several years. In the meantime renewed efforts to get the *Jupiter* signed, sealed and in the union bag persisted, often with acrimonious conflicts between the crew and organizers at the steamer's ports of call.

Some fleets, although organized, were reluctant to engage in annual negotiating sessions in which, they felt, continuing demands would inevitably escalate costs beyond reason, particularly in the era after hostilities ceased. In June of 1946, when World War II was over, Frank Jones, contract director for the N.M.U., filed notice of intent to call a strike in the fleets of seven Great Lakes operators, including the Jupiter Steamship Company. Three of the affected companies responded with the charge that it was really the union which had refused to bargain realistically and that a strike would be a direct violation of the existing contracts. To the sailors who went about their work far from the melodramas and fist poundings at the bargaining tables, it was somewhat mysterious and baffling.

The season of 1947 found the *Jupiter* still earning her keep in this, her forty-sixth season of toil, and again the object of an organizational drive by the union. Her owners, in view of several rejections of N.M.U. representation in shipboard elections, were adamant in their unwillingness to continue what they considered to be a farce. In mid-summer Captain Greenway was replaced by Captain Floyd Dossett. Bitterness reigned all through the summer. Early in the fall, however, the union apparently decided on a now-or-never campaign to bring the *Jupiter* into the fold once and for all. Pickets in unusual numbers materialized whenever the steamer was scheduled to load or unload. Puzzled dock workers, without instructions from their own union, sometimes ignored the pickets and on other occasions expressed a reluctance to "work" her, in which event the *Jupiter* would back from the dock and steam away to some alternative destination where the far-sighted Mr. Secord had made previous arrangements. But obviously the cat-and-mouse game could not go on forever, Mr. Secord and his fellow management team reasoned. Sooner or later, if the unionists were aware of the vessel's movements, there would come a time when there would be no port open to her and no choice would be left but another election and all the bitterness and frustrations it would generate.

Thereupon the astute Mr. Secord and Captain Dossett devised a clever plan that would deprive the N.M.U. boys of enough time to muster a significant showing of force at any given time or port, a ruse so confusing that the union leaders would never be certain of the *Jupiter*'s next cargo or destination. And because Captain Dossett received his orders daily from the front office by radio-telephone, also monitored by the union men, the plan was simplicity itself.

Mr. Secord and Captain Dossett devised a simple code of their very own, one without mumbo-jumbo or mysterious phrases. In essence, it was merely the substitution of port names for others, and a similar switching of cargo commodities. Thus, when Mr. Secord instructed Captain Dossett that a cargo of pig iron awaited him at Buffalo, the captain knew that "Buffalo" really meant Sandusky and that "pig iron" was coal. Ports of discharge were similarly transposed in name so that among other changes, "Milwaukee" became Muskegon and "Chicago" was understood to be Conneaut.

Thus began a traumatic period for the N.M.U. stalwarts. Eagerly they listened on the radio-telephone for the *Jupiter's* next anticipated port of call and rushed preparations to give her a dockside ring of pickets. But strangely, the old steamer failed to put in her scheduled appearance. A change of orders perhaps? No, any change would necessarily have had to come by the same instrument and no such discussion had been overheard. For the better part of a month the charade went on, the pickets mobilizing and awaiting a boat that was never to arrive. The plan was diabolical in its simplicity, miraculous in its effectiveness and ruinous to the morale of the N.M.U. leaders who raced ludicrously from one port to another in vain efforts to intercept the phantom ship that seemingly sailed endlessly on a mystic sea. Meanwhile, the *Jupiter* ambled along, oblivious to the curses that were hurled her way.

Newspapers became aware of the situation, made the most of it and soon the *Jupiter* became known far and wide as the "ghost ship," some likening her to Edward Everett Hale's "The Man Without a Country," but in this case it was "the ship without a port." The *Jupiter,* doubtless proud of the news space her wanderings inspired, was still hauling pig iron, salt, scrap or whatever cargoes were offered, carrying them wherever Mr. Secord dictated at her own modest, measured pace. "Where is the ghost ship?" newsmen kept asking Mr. Secord, but getting only a shrug of his shoulders and a sly wink in response. Captain Dossett, of course, was still not taking his radio-telephone instructions literally. Day after day, week after week, the stalemate continued, a hilarious spectacle for all but the participants and daily grist for the news media. The *Jupiter* was in the headlines every day.

It was inevitable that such a drama must one day end, and it did when the *Jupiter*'s owners finally agreed to still another election. Just as inevitable, too, was the result. The N.M.U. lost once more.

The old girl's first taste of fame, however late in life, was not to be her last. One early November night of that same year the *Jupiter,* Detroit to Milwaukee with salt, got caught in a thundering gale and snowstorm in upper Lake Michigan. She had scant horsepower to weather such a blow when she was in her prime, and now, forty-six years old, she was ill-prepared to withstand the seas that battered her continuously. Then the extreme twisting and flexing of the hull fractured some of her steam lines and she was practically helpless. Now every snow-lashed sea pushed her toward treacherous reefs that had claimed other victims. Should she escape the reefs there were always the sands off Ludington, Michigan, that had fatally clutched the *Novadoc* only seven years earlier.

Captain Dossett wasted little time in appealing to the Coast Guard for help, and now there was no code or hidden meanings in his assessment of a most perilous situation. There was considerable doubt, he stated, that his vessel could survive the night, assuming that she did not go ashore before morning. At 6:00 A.M. he reported that although he had been able to drop an anchor, it was dragging and there was some question as to whether the *Jupiter* would last out the hour.

At the first distress call the Coast Guard had requested the two nearest available vessels to stand by and render whatever assistance they found practical and possible. They were the big, clumsy but eminently seaworthy Pere Marquette carferries *City of Saginaw* and *City of Flint*. But they were high, adversely affected by the gale winds and could do little but circle the besieged freighter. At one point the *City of Saginaw* maneuvered to within a hundred feet of the *Jupiter*, but just as a line was being thrown, a huge sea hurled her around, seriously injuring one of the carferry's seamen, Frank Polasch. No further attempts to connect were made. Meanwhile, the *Jupiter*, tethered to her anchor, was taking in water as the wind swung her in almost complete circles.

The carferries were simply a stop-gap measure, insurance that the steamer's crew, or some of them, might be rescued should she go down. As soon as Captain Dossett had initiated his first distress message, the Coast Guard had alerted and dispatched the 150-foot cutter *Sundew*, from St. Joseph, Michigan. But St. Joseph was 150 miles south of Ludington and the journey was bound to be slow as the little cutter butted into big-head seas all the way. Many doubted that she would arrive in time to save the *Jupiter*. There was a slight slackening in the wind with the coming of day and at 7:00 A.M. the wallowing steamer radioed that she might possibly hold out until the cutter got there.

Shortly before noon the *Sundew*, spewing seas up and over her bow and bridge, hove on the scene. With the carferries maneuvering to give her a bit of lee, she skillfully inched in toward the *Jupiter*. She showed a magnificent disregard for the now renewed fury of the gale and the fact that heavy intermittent snow squalls momentarily left each of the four vessels out of visual touch with each other. Bravely the *Sundew* drove in as close to the stricken steamer as she could, and the first shot from her line gun put a light rope directly across the *Jupiter*'s bow. In moments a hawser was fed out from the cutter's stern and made fast. Slowly, as the *Jupiter* hoisted her anchor, the *Sundew* took up the slack and when the hawser was bar tight began dragging the *Jupiter* from the frothing shoal waters that loomed so near. Then, as the carferries blew loud and hoarse signals of "well done," the *Sundew* set about the job of towing her rescued storm victim to Milwaukee, which was where she had been bound anyway.

The *Jupiter* sailed on for another ten years and one of her last assignments, after she was sold to Cargo Carriers, Inc., and with Captain Ness Matthews in command, was the hauling of soy beans and wheat from Michigan City, Indiana, to Chicago, a distance of only thirty-five miles. Yet, when sailors spotted her, she was never just the *Jupiter*. She was that harried phantom ship that had steamed wraith-like in and out of many ports, seeking succor from her human tormentors. Her former owners, the Jupiter Steamship Company, had acquired other vessels in the intervening years, the *Malietoa,* the *Neptune,* and the *Cornell*. All had their individual histories, sometimes thrilling. But none had the fame and drama that came at a matronly age to the *Jupiter*. For she was the famous "ghost ship."

# 7

## The Reluctant Lady of McGarvey Shoal

WHEN HENRY M. FLAGLER persuaded his father-in-law, Stephen V. Harkness, to join John D. Rockefeller and a small but select group of Clevelanders in organizing and incorporating the Standard Oil Company, the gratifying events that were to transpire could scarcely have been anticipated, either by Rockefeller, Harkness or the others involved—Flagler, Samuel Andrews and William Rockefeller. The year was 1870. Canny John D. was running the show, and although the company's supply of crude oil was in Pennsylvania, the refinery was in Cleveland, which quickly became the oil capital of the world. It was like tapping the mother lode of the Comstock Mine. So astounding was the growth of the firm and so rapidly did its tentacles spread out to acquire competitors' assets and establish subsidiaries and allied corporations, all of which paid dividends to the original investors, that generations of Harknesses, Flaglers, Andrewses and Rockefellers had frequent occasions to rub their hands, shake their heads admiringly and comment most favorably on the sagacity of the old gentlemen.

McGarvey Shoal

Final rest for the Gunilda?

The almost instant prosperity of the Standard Oil Company soon dictated that the energies of its founders would henceforth be largely occupied by its financial management and the organizational intricacies of many interlocking and complementary subsidiary firms. Since New York was the corporate headquarters of the major industrial complexes and the financial capital of the country, it followed that one or more of the mushrooming Cleveland company's financial geniuses should take up legal residence there. This John D.

Rockefeller did in 1882. So assiduously did he apply himself to his tasks that before long he was reputed to be a billionaire, the richest man in the world. It follows, too, that the astute men who helped him organize the oil empire prospered accordingly.

When Stephen V. Harkness died in 1896 a Cleveland newspaper reported his estate valued at $37 million, much of it left to his son, William Lamont Harkness, of New York, who thereafter devoted his considerable talents to management of the estate. Fortunately, the rigors of the New York financial and social worlds left Mr. Harkness with ample free time to pursue his favorite hobby, yachting. This enthusiasm was shared by other members of the Harkness clan, if one judges from the pages of *Lloyd's Register of Yachts* and the roster of the New York Yacht Club in the early 1900s, before the excessive demands of the Bureau of Internal Revenue became a regrettable fact of life. Three luxury yachts were listed by *Lloyd's* as belonging to various members of the Harkness family, all sharing common characteristics. They were of steel, each powered by coal-burning steam plants. All had originated on the ways of some of the world's finest shipbuilders, in Leith, Scotland. William Lamont Harkness' *Gunilda* was 195 feet long with a gross tonnage of 385. The *Agawa,* owned by Charles W. Harkness, was 186 feet long and grossed 602 tons. Then there was Lamon V. Harkness' *Wakiva,* a thundering big 213-footer with a registered tonnage of 852. One other similarity would strike the casual peruser of such statistics—all would require professional officers and a crew of considerable numbers.

But it is William Lamont Harkness and the *Gunilda* that concerns us in this story—one that takes place not in some

*Photo from the Milton J. Brown collection*

*Victim of a Lake Huron collision in 1915, the* Choctaw *was a sister ship of the* Andaste, *lost with all hands on Lake Michigan in 1929.*

*The winter before she rammed and sank the* Choctaw, *the ice-covered* Wahcondah *was photographed at Fort William, Ontario, after a cold Lake Superior voyage.*

*Photo from the author's collection*

*Photo from the author's collection*

*At the peak of her career, the* Wolverine, *(ex-U.S.S.* Michigan) *is shown in 1913 when she toured the lakes as a training vessel . . . 70 years old and still a great lady.*

*Photo from the author's collection*

*Now moored for eternity in Erie, Pennsylvania, her home port, the bow of the Navy's first iron-hulled vessel still displays her pleasing clipper ship lines. Originally the U.S.S. Michigan, she was scorned by the service she served so well and for so long.*

Cleveland Plain Dealer *photo*

*Shown here departing Cleveland on a happy summer excursion, the* Seeandbee, *largest passenger vessel on the Great Lakes, was converted into a practice aircraft carrier during World War II.*

*The* Wolverine's *name was given to this freshwater practice aircraft carrier, a conversion of the old Great Lakes passenger vessel* Seeandbee.

*Photo from the author's collection*

*To wrench her from her bed of mud the wreckers have removed much of the old* Wolverine's *superstructure and sidewheels.*

*Still graceful, lovely and defiant. The old* Wolverine *goes to the wrecker's yard at last. The photo was taken moments before she rammed and sunk the launch.*

*Photo from the author's collection*

Photos courtesy Georgia S. Cann

*The* Hunter Savidge *in happier days, moored to a dock, probably at Alpena. Inset is Captain Fred Sharpsteen.*

Photo by McDow

*Trim and loaded with iron ore, the* William B. Davock *is shown not long before she vanished in the great Armistice Day storm of 1940.*

*In her day the ill-fated* Anna C. Minch *carried a variety of cargoes. Here she is in Cleveland with a load of pulpwood.*

Photo from the author's collection

*Photo from the Milton J. Brown collection*

*Helpless, her steam lines fractured, the* Sinaloa *was an early victim of the Armistice Day storm, driving hard on a reef at Sac Bay, on the Garden Peninsula of upper Lake Michigan.*

*Disabled and her rudder damaged, the* Conneaut *stranded on the north shore of Lake Michigan, near the Straits of Mackinac during the Armistice Day storm of 1940.*

*Photo from the author's collection*

Photo courtesy **Muskegon Chronicle**

*Broken and festooned with ice, the battered* Novadoc *lies off Juniper Beach a few days after the seas had subsided.*

*Tanker* Crudoil, *long overdue and considered lost in the Armistice Day storm of 1940, had taken shelter behind an island and survived, although damaged considerably.*

*Photo from the author's collection*

*Photo from the author's collection*

*So badly mauled was the* W. H. McGean *in the Armistice Day storm of 1940 that the crew had resigned themselves to going down with their boat.*

*Her pilot house damaged and perilously close to foundering, the* Henry Steinbrenner *limped into Chicago for extensive repairs.*

*Photo from the author's collection*

*Photo from the Milton J. Brown collection*

*All was peaceful here as the* Jupiter, *the wandering "ghost" of the Great Lakes, prepares to take on a cargo under the coal dumper.*

*Tethered to the Coast Guard Cutter* Sundew, *the disabled* Jupiter *is dragged safely away from threatening shoals in Lake Michigan in a fall storm in 1947.*

*Photo from the author's collection*

Wreck photo courtesy Oscar Anderson

*The palatial Gunilda "hard on" at McGarvey Shoal. Left inset, King Hague whose ghost still guards the wreck. Right inset, Fred Broennle who still plans to raise the yacht from 300 feet of water in Nipigon Bay.*

*McKenzie photo from Milton J. Brown collection*

*When she was launched, the* Henry Cort *had the clean cigar-shape of a typical whaleback, a profile she maintained for many years. Here she is leaving Duluth.*

*By improvised breeches buoy, the crew leaves the* Henry Cort *the morning after she was impaled and sunk on the north breakwater at Muskegon, Michigan.*

Muskegon Chronicle *photo*

Muskegon Chronicle *photo*

*Roped together for safety, the crew of the* Henry Cort *make their perilous walk to shore on the ice-sheathed breakwater.*

*Safely ashore but cold and exhausted, the crewmen of the wrecked* Henry Cort *take stock of their situation.*

Muskegon Chronicle *photo*

OPPOSITE: *Before ending her days in the boneyard, the* J. T. Reid, *sister ship of the* Henry Cort, *spent some time in the automobile trade.*

*Considerably altered from her original profile and her deck cluttered with cranes, the* Henry Cort *looked like this in her final years.*

Photo from the author's collection

*Photo from the author's collection*

*Photo by Edwin Wilson*

*The* James H. Reed *foundered moments after colliding with the* Ashcroft *on Lake Erie. Many perished but third engineer Alfred Spragge, inset, was lucky.*

*In the seductive calm of the morning after, what was left of the dismembered* Mineral State *lay off Port Stanley, Ontario, another victim of the "clay banks."*

*Photo courtesy Frank Prothero*

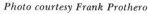

plush saltwater Shangri-La of the social set, but far up in
Lake Superior, in lonely, beautiful, island-studded Nipigon
Bay. It is a story that reveals the idiosyncrasies of mortal
man, however wealthy—a story which was without tragedy
until August of 1970.

It begins, really, in the summer of 1910 when Mr. Harkness brought the *Gunilda* to the Great Lakes by way of the St.
Lawrence River, Lake Ontario and the Welland Canal. A
former Clevelander, Harkness moored his yacht at the city's
municipal pier while he visited friends and business associates. Then, with a party of guests aboard, the *Gunilda*
departed for a leisurely cruise of the upper lakes, a trip so
relaxing and pleasant that, after departing Duluth, Mr. Harkness vowed to return the following year, allowing enough
time to go vagabonding along Lake Superior's rugged and
hauntingly lovely north shore, stopping wherever the fancy
seized him.

True to his word, the financier brought the *Gunilda* back
to the lakes in midsummer of 1911, fully prepared to explore
the Lake Superior country as it pleased him. Aboard, in addition to Mr. Harkness and his wife, Edith Hale Harkness,
and their children, Louise, thirteen, and William, eleven,
were Mr. and Mrs. J. Horace Harding, of New York, and
their son. It was a thoroughly delightful trip, with the
weather so warm that Captain Alexander Corkum had the
crew put up the deck awnings early in the voyage. Ranging
along the north shore, the crew and guests were treated to
some of the most spectacular scenery in North America, an
enchanting wilderness broken only by the flashing navigational lights at Coppermine Point, Cape Gargantua,
Michipicoten Island, Otter Island and Peninsula Harbor.

Wherever it pleased him, Harkness would order the yacht anchored, usually in some picturesque spot where both scenery and fishing were good. One such anchorage was in little Port Coldwell harbor where the Gerow family, father and six sons, were commercial fishermen. Henry Gerow, ten years old at the time, still recalls the *Gunilda* as the most beautiful vessel he has ever seen. "She was painted white," he recalls. "The brass fittings on her decks and superstructure were so highly polished that when the sun came out, the glitter almost stole the show."

While at Port Coldwell some of the crew went ashore to visit the little store near the Canadian Pacific Railway line to purchase milk, eggs and vegetables from Gerow's mother.

It was at Port Coldwell that Captain Corkum evinced his first qualms about proceeding into Nipigon Bay, which Harkness desired to cruise, without the services of a knowledgeable local pilot. Inquiries ashore brought an offer from Donald Murray, a thoroughly experienced man, to pilot the *Gunilda* into Nipigon Bay and the village of Rossport for the sum of fifteen dollars. But Harkness, in control of one of America's great fortunes and with a one-hundred-thousand-dollar yacht under his feet, apparently thought the figure mentioned was entirely too high and brusquely rejected the offer.

The next day, as the *Gunilda* was coaling at Jackfish Bay, the last stop before the Nipigon Bay adventure, similar inquiries inspired a proposal from one Harry Legault that he pilot the vessel as far as Rossport in return for twenty-five dollars and his train fare back to Jackfish Bay. Outraged at what he considered to be a preposterous fee, although it struck Captain Corkum and others as entirely reasonable, Harkness dismissed the whole idea.

The *Gunilda* was adequately supplied with charts of the area, but they were, of course, American charts. While they were substantially identical with Canadian charts of the same areas, there were, Captain Corkum knew, subtle differences and probably some hazards known only to the commercial fishermen whose intimate knowledge of specific areas would put the chartmakers' skills to shame. However, he was confident that with caution the *Gunilda* would come to no harm.

There are five ship channels leading into Nipigon Bay–Nipigon Strait, Moffat Strait, Simpson Channel, Wilson Channel, and the Schreiber, or North, Channel. Schreiber Channel, the first they would encounter from the direction of their approach, was chosen by Captain Corkum as the logical course. A dangerous reef, nearly awash and called Bread Rock, lies near the entrance from Lake Superior, between the mainland and Copper Island. A mile beyond Copper Island, with only four feet of water over it, and unmarked is McGarvey Shoal, a peak of granite that rises from a depth of three hundred feet. In local fishermen's parlance it is known as "Old Man's Hump." Bread Rock was buoyed and clearly marked on the *Gunilda*'s chart, but McGarvey Shoal, although it appeared on Canadian charts, was not indicated on the American chart being used by Captain Corkum. Therefore, after making his turn into Schreiber Channel between Bread Rock and Schreiber Point, on the mainland, with the charted depths clearly indicating more than three hundred feet of water under the keel, he confidently shoved the engine telegraph to "full ahead."

The *Gunilda,* a thing of beauty, was bustling along with

a bone in her teeth and her brightwork glistening when little Joe King, helping his mother pick raspberries on nearby
Healey Island, ceased his labors to admire the scene. The sky
was dappled with fleecy clouds, the blue of Nipigon Bay
showed only a gentle chop and he thought it about the prettiest sight he had ever seen. He was still watching when the
*Gunilda* hit McGarvey Shoal.

The shock was tremendous, throwing crew and passengers
helter-skelter and clearing the pantry shelves of most of the
yacht's prized china. Sheer momentum carried her on and
up until a full eighty feet of her hull was hung over the rock
shoal, her raking clipper bow pointing skyward and her stern
angling downward until her below-deck portholes aft were a
scant two feet out of water. It would have broken the back of
a lesser vessel, but the *Gunilda* was the product of fine Scotch
shipwrights. She remained tight and dry despite the severity
of the shock and the grinding punishment her bottom plates
must have taken.

When it became apparent that the yacht was not going to
sink and the crew could be seen lowering the big launch, Joe
King and his mother continued to pick raspberries, for theirs
was a serious expedition. Dining-room stewards on the Canadian Pacific Railway usually bought their fish at Rossport,
wiring ahead so that a supply would be ready when the
trains arrived. In season, too, they would frequently request
a few baskets of the wild raspberries that grew so abundantly
on the islands of Nipigon Bay. The responsibility for filling
these orders fell to Mrs. King, and, time being of the essence,
Joe usually went along to help. They had rowed over to
Healey Island and had watched the *Gunilda* hit the shoal
from a distance of about two miles. As Joe explained fre-

quently in the days to follow, "There wasn't anything we could do, so we just went on picking berries."

By the time the Kings had rowed back to Rossport and prepared their berries, the passengers and most of the crew of the *Gunilda* were already at the station awaiting the train to Port Arthur. Mr. Harkness was sorely vexed and most anxious to wire his insurance company and make arrangements for taking his yacht off McGarvey Shoal. Both missions, however, of necessity had to wait until he reached Port Arthur or its neighboring city, Fort William, to determine what salvage and repair facilities existed. But the unusual number of passengers boarding the train at little Rossport inspired considerable gossip. By the time the train steamed out of the station, the telegraph operator had already informed his fellow operator in Port Arthur that a big yacht had been wrecked in Nipigon Bay. From the railway station in Port Arthur the news spread rapidly through the twin cities and in official circles in Fort William was greeted with incipient panic. Could it be the *Catania?*

Mayor Young and the official family of Fort William had been in a bit of a tizzy for some time over the impending arrival of the steam yacht *Catania,* the regal craft of the Duke of Sutherland. His Grace, with a party that included Lord Charles Beresford, Sir Henry Pellatt and the Hon. Arthur Stanley, brother of Lord Derby, were due on an informal inspection trip of the two cities and their common harbor, Thunder Bay. The exclusive Canadian Club and the Industrial Bureau had made hasty but impressive plans to show the area to its best advantage. The problem was that nobody knew just when the sleek *Catania* might come steaming in between Pie Island and Thunder Cape Light to catch the mayor and his welcoming committee napping.

Mayor Young, on pins and needles, had wired Captain Anderson of the *Catania,* at Toronto, asking for an exact arrival time and extending the hospitality of the city to the Duke and Lord Charles. But Captain Anderson's plans were pretty much subject to the whims of the Duke and likely to be frequently changed. Being unable to offer anything approximating an arrival date, the captain had not replied, leaving Mayor Young to stew in a porridge of nagging worries. Then there was this dreadful news of the big steam yacht piled up on McGarvey Shoal. Had the Duke decided to take a tour of lovely Nipigon Bay? Was it the *Catania?* Was all now to go for naught? Mayor Young was immensely relieved when aides hastened to him with news that the vessel involved was not the *Catania* but rather the yacht of a voluble American millionaire who was at that very moment castigating Canadian marine authorities for not marking McGarvey Shoal with a buoy, although only five years earlier the Canadian survey vessel *Bayfield,* so he had been given to understand, had come to grief on that very same shelf of granite that rose from the depths.

Johnson & Higgins, the Harkness insurance agents in New York, had already set the salvage machinery in motion by the time the yacht's owner had put his friends and family aboard the passenger steamer *Hamonic,* headed for the lower lakes and home. They had contacted Jim Whalen of the Canadian Towing and Wrecking Company, the Port Arthur firm best equipped for the job. In addition to scows, barges and ancillary gear, he owned the tug *James Whalen,* largest and most powerful on Lake Superior. As soon as he could round up a crew Whalen left for the site of the stranding, the barge *Empire,* loaded with gear, following behind the tug. Harkness, however, chose to return to Rossport by train, there hiring a fisherman to take him out to the scene as soon as the wreckers arrived.

Things normally being rather quiet in remote and secluded Nipigon Bay, a number of the citizens of Rossport and the surrounding area, welcoming the diversion, were on hand in small boats to watch the attempt to refloat the *Gunilda.* It promised to be a gala occasion, with each amateur expert in the flotilla espousing his own theory on just how the stranded yacht could best be taken off the shoal. Harkness, once he had climbed aboard the *James Whalen,* was most anxious to get the operation started.

Captain Whalen, after probing the existing water on both sides of the *Gunilda,* found that she had rammed so forcefully up on the granite shelf that there was only five feet of water under her hull at a point where she normally drew more than twelve feet. Captain Whalen, who had originally anticipated no more than a more-or-less routine hauling-off job, was concerned over the possibility of the yacht heeling to one side or the other once the tug put a strain on the line and the wash from her thirteen-foot propeller provided lift to the stern of the *Gunilda.*

The verbal exchanges between the Captain and Harkness are still recalled by some who were on the scene that fateful morning, and the memories often inspire great thigh-slapping guffaws. The millionaire yachtsman, who had spurned the services of a pilot because he considered the proposed fifteen-dollar fee exorbitant, apparently suffered from an af-

fliction common to people in his position—the philosophy
that everybody was out to "take" him.[1]

Captain Whalen, noting the extreme angle of the hull, her
bow rearing high out of the water, her stern far down, was
extremely hesitant about attempting a straight pull.

"I think," said Captain Whalen, "that I should go back to
Port Arthur and get two scows. We could lash one to each
side of the yacht and put a heavy chain between them, under
the hull of the *Gunilda*. That way, if she decides to misbe-
have, she will be supported aft and come to no harm."

Harkness, envisioning the plan as an excuse to make the
salvage operation more costly, and expressing himself freely
on the point, was adamant. "She went on straight and she'll
come off straight. Just pull!"

"She's on an even keel now," admitted Whalen, "but
there's no telling what will happen when she begins to move.
She ought to have support aft."

"Never mind that," snapped Harkness; "just pull her off."

With wisdom based on experience, Captain Whalen had
his men carry a twelve-inch hawser from the tug around the
yacht, passing it through the hawse pipes and securing it to
the *Gunilda*'s fore bitts. Two steel towing cables were made
fast from the tug's bitts to those on the aft end of the
stranded yacht. All was ready.

"I still think we ought to have a couple of scows lashed to
her," grumbled Captain Whalen.

"Pull, just pull," growled Harkness.

"But suppose she lists or twists?" argued Whalen.

"Pull, man, pull!"

Captain Whalen put the tug on half-ahead, increasing the
strain steadily as the lines grew bar-tight, until the telegraph

registered full ahead. If there was any sign of movement on the part of the yacht, it was imperceptible. After fifteen minutes the tug's engine was checked down, finally stopped. In an attempt to provide even more lift from the wash of the big propeller, the captain ordered the lines shortened, bringing the stern of the tug closer to the *Gunilda*. Again the *James Whalen* took a strain on the lines and worked ahead with maximum effort on the part of her big engine. No progress being observed, Captain Whalen swung the wheel to one side, then the other, hoping the seesaw motion would inspire some response. And, ever so slowly, it did.

"She's moving," shouted one of the deck crew.

But instead of sliding evenly on her bed of granite, the *Gunilda* groaned, slid back only slightly and almost immediately took a heavy list to starboard, putting her after rail under water. So simple and straightforward had the salvage operation seemed that nobody had thought to close her portholes or secure her companionway doors. Drinking in the cold waters of Nipigon Bay in big gulps, the *Gunilda* filled, not rapidly, but steadily. Her bow, already at an extremely raking angle skyward, increased that angle as the after end slid slowly under, her progress downward noted by geysers of water as compression blew out her portholes, companionways, hatches and engine-room skylight. Tug crewmen, acting instinctively, grabbed axes and severed the tow lines to keep their vessel from being drawn down too.

It was all over in a few minutes. Where once had rested a palatial yacht, there was now only disturbed water, a succession of big bubbles and what floated off as she disappeared in three hundred feet of water—a naphtha launch, a cutter, a small sailing boat, dinghy and a couple dozen wooden steamer chairs. The end had come so suddenly that observers in the armada of small boats could only gasp in surprise and amazement. Many wondered why, since the insurance underwriters would be absorbing the salvage costs in any event, the yachtsman had spurned the considered advice of an expert salvager?

William Lamont Harkness, standing on the stern of the tug as his beloved *Gunilda* vanished in a lather of white water and a massive eruption of air bubbles, was philosophic as well behooves a man who had overruled an expert and harvested himself a crop of disaster.

According to some who were on the tug that day, Harkness shrugged his shoulders somewhat sheepishly and said to Captain Whalen, "Well, they're still building more just like her."

Over the years, as the *Gunilda* has lain beckoningly at the foot of the granite peak that is McGarvey Shoal, her bow in three hundred feet of water, she has inspired some fantastic treasure yarns. The very fact that she was owned by a multimillionaire spawned stories of riches beyond belief—of a solid silver service worth $250,000, of priceless and exquisite china, rare vintage wine and spirits and a fortune in jewels and cash in her safe. As always, when a wreck lies silent and tantalizingly out of reach, when treasure tales are told and retold, the riches within the hulk are inflated beyond reason or probability.

A realistic appraisal of the times, facts and known circumstances would discount many of the treasure fables and bring others into more reasonable perspective. One yarn, for example, hangs on the rumor that insurance claims of $3,500,000 were paid for jewels, cash and personal property that went down with the yacht. Had such a reputed fortune in jewels and cash reposed in the *Gunilda's* safe, the insurance companies would most certainly have made an attempt to recover at least a portion of their losses. The valuation would have justified mounting a full-scale salvage operation by competent specialists. And common sense would rule out the probability of either the Harknesses or their guests taking the family jewels or a significant amount of money along on a vagabonding cruise of Lake Superior. Louise Harkness (now Mrs. David S. Ingalls), thirteen at the time and the only surviving member of the owner's party on the *Gunilda* that day, confirms that there was nothing of great value aboard, only personal belongings.

Despite all assurances to the contrary, the belief still exists that untold riches lie deep down off McGarvey Shoal and nearly every summer there is talk of a proposed salvage expedition to retrieve the treasures. Some, taking the treasure yarns with several grains of salt, would be satisfied with some important memento or relic—the *Gunilda's* bell, the three-inch brass saluting cannons mounted on her bridge wings or one of her headboards with the heavy cast-brass letters spelling out her name. For most, however, the extreme depth has ruled out the possibility of their dreams becoming reality.

For years the *Gunilda* challenged the imagination of Ed Flatt, of Port Arthur. Knowledge of the yacht's position led him to believe that he could raise her by using big grappling hooks suspended by cables working from winches on the deck of a barge he acquired. The *Gunilda*, as it has been with many, became an obsession with Flatt. While many might disagree with his technique, they could not fault his determination and enthusiasm. Strangely, Flatt was the first one to bring up a souvenir from the long-sunken yacht. He was successful in hooking the foremast of the *Gunilda* and breaking off the top third, with the masthead lights still intact. The mast was towed to Rossport, where today it is mounted near Rossport Inn, a fisherman's resort paradise operated by Toivo Seppala. The pulleys were still as free as the day they were placed on the yacht, and when current was applied to the broken electrical wires, the masthead lights went on! It was Seppala's father-in-law, Oscar Anderson, who had the foresight to photograph the *Gunilda* as she hung there on the shoal on August 30, 1911.

In the early 1960s a Port Arthur hard-hat diver named Jack Coghlan, succumbing to the lure of the *Gunilda* and the $250,000 in silverware and jewelry he was convinced were still in her, made two attempts to reach the hull. Working from the boat of a local marina and charter boat operator, Ray Kenney, Coghlan reported symptoms of nitrogen narcosis at a depth of one hundred and fifty feet and had to abandon his quest.

Next to seek the fabled yacht was Chuck Zehnder, a former Minneapolis resident, scuba diver and long a student of Lake Superior shipwreck lore. He arrived over the *Gunilda*'s grave in August of 1969, fifty-eight years after the sinking. His experience, research and personal enthusiasm had inspired the loan of needed equipment by several companies—a houseboat, sonar gear, special rope, additional diving gear and underwater lights. With Zehnder was his wife Sandi, also an experienced scuba diver, and Mr. and Mrs. John Golden of New Bruno, New Jersey. Golden, an army buddy of Zehnder, had also racked up considerable time underwater. But Lake Superior presents special problems due to its perpetual low temperatures. Even in August it is frightfully cold—thirty-four degrees at the depth of the *Gunilda*.

"With Ed Flatt to pinpoint the area of search, we located the wreck by sonar," recalls Zehnder. "A big kedge anchor was hung over the side of the houseboat and the craft permitted to drift until the anchor caught and set herself somewhere on the *Gunilda*'s superstructure or rigging. Then, getting into my scuba gear, I went over the side, on this first trip without lights or equipment.

"Two minutes after leaving the surface I reached her bow at about 270 feet. I remained there long enough to determine it was the ship and that our buoy rope would not pull free. The total dive time was twelve minutes."

Bad weather kept the divers dock-bound at Rossport for three days and it was August 9 when next they moored over the wreck.

"It was time for a second attempt to reach the yacht," says Zehnder. "This time I took lights and some tools, actually only a pry bar and hacksaw. I hoped to remain on board long enough to get the bell which is right up on the bow, but had to do it in only twelve minutes from the time I left the surface because of the combination of water temperature and decompression. At 225 feet my diving light was crushed completely, including the battery, and I became unnerved. I was feeling little effects of nitrogen narcosis, but pure unadulterated fear. I had only been to 200 feet once before and that was in the clear waters off Oahu, in Hawaii, eight years before, so this cold darkness at well below 200 feet was something to respect. I rationalized that I wouldn't be able to see the bell or the yacht without the light and headed for the choppy surface, nearly twenty-five stories away. I was already convinced that more rugged and sophisticated equipment would be needed to do any significant salvage work, even the recovery of artifacts. But I left, reluctantly, vowing to return another day."

A year from the day of Zehnder's second descent, on August 9, 1970, the cold dark hull of the *Gunilda* claimed its only victim, twenty-three-year-old Charles King Hague, better known simply as King. Hague was recognized as one of the top scuba experts in the Thunder Bay area. He was one of a party that included his wife Maria; Art Joseph, a Thunder Bay police officer; Fred and Sandy Broennle and their son Mark, all in Broennle's salvage boat *Lady-Go-Diver*. Broennle, another recognized diving authority, had built the boat specifically for diving and salvage work.

On the approximate wreck site Broennle started to run sonar graphs of the entire area as King Hague and young Mark, working from a sixteen-foot aluminum skiff, dragged with grappling hooks. During this operation, a submerged buoy was discovered four feet below the surface and anchored in eighty feet of water. At the same time the sonar began to pick up the distinct outline of a wreck, below the 300-foot mark. At almost this same instant Hague called out that he had hooked into something at the 125-foot level. Broennle joined the pair in the small boat after Hague had suited up. But the underwater mystery was solved quickly, with Hague registering obvious disappointment when he found the grapple merely caught in a crevice of the nearly vertical rock shoal. Then he decided to look at the anchor on the submerged buoy.

"I told him to wait until I got suited up," Broennle recalls with great sadness. "But he just said that he would be back up before we could row back to the *Lady-Go-Diver* and that I should forget it. With these words he disappeared. I watched his bubbles. He hung around the bottom of the eighty-foot drop for half a minute and what happened after that sent a chill through me. The air bubbles started to move away from the anchor chain of the buoy, in the direction of the *Lady-Go-Diver*. Looking at his exhaust bubbles, I realized he was getting into deep water, too deep for anybody diving on compressed air. As a diver descends his bubbles reaching the surface become smaller and more dispersed the deeper he goes, like a huge gin fizz. I followed the clouds of bursting bubbles in the direction of the *Lady-Go-Diver* and I knew King was in trouble. It was just like a nightmare. King was now in approximately 300 feet of water, his exhaust bubbles taking several minutes to reach the surface. By the time they broke the surface he might be fifty yards away and moving in a different direction. By now he had to be completely out of air, according to my calculations. Forty feet past the stern of the salvage boat he swam a complete circle and headed in an easterly direction. The straight line he took from the buoy would indicate that he was following a sunken cable to the wreck."

At that instant Broennle caught a glimpse of something just below the surface and grabbed it. It was Hague's dive light, covered with mud and rust but still burning. Frantically climbing into his own gear he shot down the anchor chain of the buoy and down the rock wall of the shoal. At 180 feet he leveled off, hanging on to the rock while he tried to inflate his life jacket to retain neutral buoyancy. His wet suit, once three-eighths of an inch thick, was now compressed paper thin, and the thirty pounds of weights which had maintained neutral buoyancy at the surface were now pulling him down. He managed to get a few puffs of air into his life jacket when he slipped off the ledge and fell, the face mask now squashed against his face. Seconds later he found himself kneeling in what appeared to be clay and steel cables, probably the ones used in the attempt to pull the *Gunilda* off McGarvey Shoal! And there, right in front of him was the bow of the long-sought luxury yacht. But now his mask was filling with blood from burst blood vessels in his left eye and nose.

"But I was feeling the effect of nitrogen narcosis," says Broennle. "Today, when I think back at the happy feeling I had when I saw the bow of the *Gunilda* there is no explanation of what made me literally climb up the cliff toward the surface instead of inspecting the *Gunilda* and looking for King. At sixty feet my slightly inflated life jacket started to give me positive buoyancy. I don't remember much after that for at fifty feet I ran out of air. When I came to, the blue sky was above me, as were the faces of Mark and Maria who were dragging me back to the boat."

Broennle tried once more but again, this time at only sixty feet, his mask began to fill with blood. He would have made still another attempt but was restrained by Art Joseph.

Dragging operations by the Ontario Provincial Police were not successful, and a host of diving friends who volunteered their services were dissuaded from risking their lives in further efforts to recover the body.

"It was a hard decision to come to," sighed Maria Hague. "But I finally decided that it would be best to leave King where he was. He was in his environment. We often spoke of how we would choose to go if we had to. He said he would like to die diving on a wreck and that he wouldn't want to be recovered. He had gotten his wish and I didn't want to ruin it!"

During the next few days Broennle did some soul search-ing which ended in his firm resolve to return to the *Gunilda* some day, but with more deep-water knowledge and sophis-ticated equipment. And many things have happened since that tragic day off McGarvey Shoal.

"I felt that the *Gunilda* owed me something," he philoso-phizes, "or maybe I felt that I owed her something."

Giving up his electrical contracting business, he formed his own salvage company, Deep Diving Systems Ltd. Two local business men, Cecil Eade and Dave McBlain, agreed to help with the financing and give other practical assistance. A total of $25,000 was needed to purchase a CCR-1000 Re-Breather, a hot-water suit, a boiler and a decompression chamber. They also built a diving bell to act as an under-water stage for decompression stops. To gain the more special-ized knowledge of deep-compression diving Broennle toured the United States from one end to the other, spending three weeks at San Diego with underwater experts working on off-shore drilling platforms. Another three weeks was invested at Philadelphia's BioMarine Industries, working with Fred Parker, inventor of the CCR-1000 closed-circuit re-breather. The decompression chamber he found in Louisiana where he had to build a trailer to haul it home. Prior to this he vis-ited London for official clearance from Lloyd's and got per-mission for the project from the Dominion's Receiver of Wrecks.

In August of 1971 the salvage crew moored their equip-ment-laden barge over the *Gunilda* after several experimental dives to perfect the system and techniques. Broennle left the deck of the barge shortly after three o'clock one afternoon. On his way down he passed backup diver Dennis Kotyk, stationed on the diving-bell platform at the 110-foot level. A communications system enabled· those topside to know exactly what the diver was doing.

"Then I spotted her," Broennle relates, "sitting almost level and looking surprisingly fit. I was so happy I went over and kissed the mast. I landed on her stern, near the engine-room hatch. I only stayed on the ship for five minutes, but to prove I had made a successful journey I got one of the skylight vents and brought it back with me. It proved to be all brass."

"Any time you do anything of this magnitude it has to be a team effort," Broennle emphasizes. "Dave McBlain was the decompression supervisor and Cecil Eade looked after the boiler, temperature control and winches. Gene Medeo handled the hot-water supply to the suit and Ian McCool, our second backup diver, also handled the communications. The diving bell, which worked perfectly, was designed by Maurice Helie. At the depth we were working, everything was a 'first' for Lake Superior."

Broennle made one more exploratory dive before the salvage team left the site. "I went into the engine room and stayed on the observation platform. I didn't go all over the ship. We aren't looking for any treasures just yet. There is plenty of work to do before this happens and, as I have always maintained, we won't rush this project."

Broennle eventually plans to lift the *Gunilda* with twelve big air bags, each with a lifting capability of forty-five tons and stationed strategically on a "cradle" around the hull.

When the lift has been deemed successful the *Gunilda* will still be fifty feet below the surface, but will then be towed up the steamboat channel into Kopkii Bay for final refloating.

But air bags and other myriad ancillary gear needed for a major salvage job are expensive and take time to make or acquire. Nevertheless, the indomitable Broennle keeps on working and planning for the day when big compressors will begin to fill the air bags until the *Gunilda* grows restless at her silted bottom moorings.

So there the fabulous *Gunilda* lies, with her secrets still safe from those who would seek her rumored treasures. But the lure of sunken riches has been known to overpower reasonable and considered thought. Ten men died trying to get the copper from the hulk of the old *Pewabic*, in Lake Huron, and others have perished in ill-fated salvage expeditions all over the Great Lakes. But when Fred Broennle, who is a reasoned and considered man, next descends into the gloom that exists at over three hundred feet at the bottom of McGarvey Shoal, he will be watched and cheered by the ghost of the man who now guards the hulk of the tantalizing *Gunilda,* Charles King Hague!

---

[1] While William L. Harkness' sensitivity in monetary situations in which he was apprehensive about being "taken" by opportunistic individuals was perhaps understandable, he was not adverse to philanthropic endeavors when the cause was clear-cut and worthy. As an alumnus of Yale University he bestowed upon his alma mater some $400,000 for the construction of the Harkness Quadrangle, among other ancillary facilities. Another Harkness gift, in conjunction with Mrs. Harkness, was $25,000 for the establishment, in Cleveland, in 1899, of the Rainbow Cottage for Crippled and Convalescent Children, which evolved, eventually, into Rainbow Babies and Childrens Hospital, now part of Cleveland's justly famed University Hospitals.

# 8

## *"To Hell With 'er!"*

ANY NUMBER OF PEOPLE, most or all of them sailors, can testify that vessels, like the ladies they are said to personify, occasionally develop petulant and unpredictable dispositions once the golden days of youth are behind them. Such a craft was the *Henry Cort,* and all boats are "she" despite whatever names might be lettered across their bows. Always a steady, hard-working lady, she had some lively times for twenty-five years before a change in deportment. Some say it was because too much was asked of her, that she simply rebelled against the unreasonable demands of her owners after a quarter-century of practically unblemished service. Others were inclined to think that she deeply resented the structural changes or "face lift" that later altered the profile, features and trim she had enjoyed in the good days. And there were still a few who swore that, being a sensitive lady, she deplored the turn of events that eventually took her from the fresh free winds on the long hauls of ore and grain from the upper lakes to Lake Erie, and put her instead in the tramp trade, carrying pig iron, scrap, slag and heaven-knows-what, always ending up in some evil-smelling backwater dock wreathed in the noxious fumes of foundry furnaces.

Be that as it may, it is a matter of record that her last seventeen years, although she was still only middle-aged as lakes vessel statistics are reckoned, were fraught with misfortune, calamity and travail. It is also a matter of record that her chief engineer for her last seven years, August "Augie" Britz, put up with her temper tantrums and cantankerous behavior above and beyond the call of duty. It may have been that in the seven years an inevitable affection developed between man and the machinery put in his care, a romance easily understandable to a mechanically inclined individual. But more likely it was just the standard philosophy of owners who kept their engineers assigned to the old triple-expansion mills they knew so well, on the theory that efficiency and economy could best be achieved by trusting the operation of the engines to men who knew their every whim and mood. Captains frequently moved from boat to boat, but engineers seemed forever wedded to their engines. Augie Britz, who hailed from Marine City, Michigan, and a long line of engineers, was such a man.

Born the *Pillsbury* in the McDougall yard at Superior, Wisconsin, as one of the distinctive whaleback types her builder made famous, she was launched in 1892 as was her sister ship, the *Washburn,* both seemingly destined for the grain trade by the Pillsbury Flour Mills Company. However, both had side gangways and a 'tween-decks arrangement and began life in the package freight trade, the *Pillsbury* carrying the Soo Line insignia on her bows. But only three years after launching, both vessels were acquired by Rockefeller's Bessemer Steamship Company and renamed, the *Pillsbury* becoming the *Henry Cort,* the *Washburn,* the *James B. Neil-son.*[1] It was an era of great change and financial conflict on the iron ranges of Minnesota and Wisconsin, with men of much vision and even more money jockeying for position and supremacy, calling the signals from both high offices in Cleveland and on Wall Street, in New York. Only six years after losing the original owners and names, the *Cort* and *Neilson* became part of a gigantic financial manipulation when the entire Bessemer fleet was taken over by the even larger Pittsburgh Steamship Company fleet, but this time without losing their names.

Until 1917 the *Cort* seemed to enjoy the role for which she was destined, hauling about 3000 long tons of iron ore from the American lakehead to steel plants along the south shore of Lake Erie or unloading at transfer ports where her cargo would be forwarded by rail to inland mills. On the return trips her cargo was often coal for Superior or Duluth, with only a very occasional shift to the grain trade when these late-season cargoes were highly profitable. Only once did she suffer an unusually heavy mauling by the seas and that was in the "Big Blow" of 1913 when tremendous following gray-beards buckled in the turrets that supported her after house, plucked away her sidelights and even relieved her of her headlight, mounted high on the forward spar. A lesser vessel would have succumbed to the punishment the *Cort* took that day.

When she was only a maidenly twenty-five years old, and some say it was the exigencies of war that prompted it, the *Cort* first began to exhibit the reprehensible characteristics for which she was later to become best known. Nineteen-seventeen saw the third year of the great conflict in Europe

creating peak demands for iron ore and grain both in Canada
and the United States. Worst of all, it promised to be the
bitterest winter in a decade. On December 7 the temperature
at the American lakehead was already down to twenty degrees
below zero. Heavy ice had formed all along the St. Marys, St.
Clair and Detroit rivers, and in Lake St. Clair there was a very
real danger of a score of more of cargo-laden vessels being
frozen in for the winter. Indeed, so precarious did the situation seem that for the first time in history the government
assumed the cost of massing a fleet of ice-breaking craft—big
tugs, carferries and a few conventional steamers strengthened
for ice conditions. On December 16 the prognosis was extremely grave. The stricken, ice-bound vessels were clustered
in groups up and down the connecting waterways, awaiting
the muscle and horsepower of the carferries and ice-breaking
types to break them out.

Scattered like broken straws in the jumbled floes in the
Detroit River, above Amherstburg, were the *Lakeland, Roch-
ester, Midvale, William C. Agnew, Quincey Shaw, Alexis W.
Thompson, Leonard B. Miller, Connemaugh, Rufus P. Ran-
ney, Amazon, Uranus, M. C. Smith* and *John Sherwin*. Far-
ther up the river were the *Goodyear, Luzon, Wissahicken,
A. A. Augustus, Sierra, E. N. Britung, Verona, B. F. Jones,
America, Stadaconna* and *Colonel*.

Up on the St. Clair River, at Marine City, were the *Arcturus, Theodore H. Wickwire, Yosemite, Adam E. Cornelius,
M. A. Reeb, Chicago, Buffalo, Jacob T. Kopp* and *Arthur
Orr*. And still fighting their way down the lower St. Marys
or slogging the length of Lake Huron were another two-
dozen steamers, unaware that their downbound predecessors
were ice-bound and going nowhere.

Of more immediate concern was the fact that another modest fleet was completely immobilized in heavy ice in Lake Erie, more precisely at Bar Point, at the junction with the lower Detroit River where the shipping channel, in relatively shallow water, is narrowly defined. This, in effect, made a mockery of ice-breaking efforts farther up the river, the freed vessels having literally no choice but to drop anchor and chance being frozen in again. This vital intelligence, once it was made known in shipping-firm offices and more specifically the Lake Carriers' Association, inspired immediate action. The ice, it was reported by observers, was heavier than in many years. Once heavy floes "grounded" in shallow water, untold thousands of tons of ice, driven relentlessly by the winds, rafted or windrowed, impacting and consolidating until the mass was almost impenetrable, even by the most powerful ice-breaking carferries, which were already at work in the ice in Whitefish Bay and the upper and lower St. Marys, hundreds of miles to the north. The potential for ruinous losses was very real, many owners justly fearing that their vessels would be frozen in for the winter with resultant heavy damage if not total destruction.

Harry Coulby, president of the Pittsburgh Steamship Company, with the fate of many of his own vessels at stake, immediately called Lorain to muster assistance. The *Cort* and *Neilson,* already beginning lay-up preparation, were ordered activated at once with orders to proceed to Bar Point for ice-breaking duty. Strangely, although small compared to some of the larger units of the fleet, both, by the very nature of their whaleback construction, were ideally built to break ice. The extreme rake of their spoon-shaped bows permitted them to charge ahead and ride right up on the ice, crushing it down by their very weight. The crews were naturally unhappy, but it was an emergency situation, so out of Lorain they charged with Captain John Murray leading the way from the pilot house of the *Cort.*

The panorama of ice-stranded vessels that greeted him at Bar Point was even more extensive than he had expected. On both sides of the accepted channel long boats were helpless, carried north and south of their courses by the force of wind-blown fields of ice. The lane through which the *Cort* had approached the scene was, strangely, still navigable but significantly narrowed. Into the fray plunged the *Cort* and *Neilson,* trying to circle the steamers closest to the channel to cut them free and send them on their way. Meanwhile, from the *Cort*'s pilot house Captain Murray could see the smoke plumes of at least a dozen vessels coming slowly down the Detroit River between Amherstburg and Grosse Ile, their masters obviously under the impression that all was clear, completely unaware of the ice-bound fleet off Bar Point. Under the existing condition, all they could do when they reached the bottleneck was to steam ahead in single file while attempting to stay in the constricted, ice-clogged channel. It was touch and go with no alternative but to go ahead. So along they came, the first contingent freed from the ice in the Detroit River—the *Lakeland, Rochester, Midvale, William C. Agnew, Quincy A. Shaw, Alexis W. Thompson, Leonard B. Miller, Connemaugh, Rufus P. Ranney, Amazon, Uranus, M. C. Smith,* and *John Sherwin,* an imposing fleet whose fate would be sealed within hours by the whims of the elements.

Captain Murray wasted not a moment. While the *Neilson* drove in between two inert, but impatient vessels, the *Cort* singled out another and ploughed her bow up on the windrows that imprisoned her. The whaleback would charge high up on the ice, break it down and then back off for another attack. And it was now that the *Cort,* doubtless sulking about having so unceremoniously ordered from comfortable winter moorings, evinced the first symptoms of a changed personality, a marked reluctance to follow orders.

In the gloom of dusk out there in the ice the first of the long line of downbound steamers from the Amherstburg Channel approached the jam off Bar Point with the *Lakeland,* the leading vessel, carefully threading the broken ice and dark streaks of water that denoted the narrowing and only path. And because they were thirteen in number, if one was inclined to be superstitious, the developing drama was fraught with all sorts of dire possibilities.

The *Cort* was still busily gnawing away at a modest windrow that imprisoned an ore-laden steamer, running ahead as far as she could go and then backing off for another go at it. The *Lakeland* passed safely astern of her as did the *Rochester.* But then came the fit of pique that was to characterize her penchant for trouble the rest of her days. Captain Murray, after jamming the *Cort*'s bow into the windrow, rang for full astern to back her off for another try. Astern she went, but so rapidly did she slide backward off a particularly troublesome hummock that the captain's frantic signal for full ahead failed to take the way off her, or at least she was uncommonly tardy in obeying. The skipper of the third vessel of the downbound armada, the 600-foot, ore-laden *Midvale,* was then horrified to see the 320-foot silhouette of the *Cort,* a long black shape in the murky dusk, slide directly across the narrow channel practically under his bows. Automatically he ran down for full astern but with no chance of taking the way off his boat before the inevitable collision with the whaleback!

Mortally holed, the *Cort* began taking aboard great gulps of water while the air was rent with the strident clamor of steamboat whistles sounding the distress signal. A Lake Erie carferry with modest horsepower, also working as an ice-breaker, quickly bulled her way upon the scene to take off the stricken steamer's crew, and none too soon. In minutes the once-docile and obedient *Henry Cort*, a victim of a single moment of shrewish behavior, was on the bottom in thirty-five feet of water, only her spars and the top of her funnel marking her new-found winter moorings! The *Neilson*, with the deportment of a perfect lady, was ordered to stand by the wreck to warn the downbound stragglers of the obstruction.

It was a foregone conclusion that the *Cort* would have to wait until spring for salvage, and her location was methodically charted by half a dozen experts. But the ice conditions on Lake Erie that winter of 1917–1918 were truly deplorable. Easterly winds piled the ice up in the shallow western basin, the driven floes sliding up on those anchored ashore and pounding the previous accumulations right down to the bottom. And when the first strong westerlies of the new season came the entire mass was driven with them, truly an irresistible force that scoured the lake bottom as the ice fields moved. In early April, when Captains F. A. Bailey and W. W. Smith, wrecking master and marine superintendent, respectively, for the Pittsburgh Steamship Company, sought to locate the *Cort* for salvage preparations she was nowhere to be found. Now with a new season about to begin and the wreck of a steamer possibly in the shipping lanes, finding and marking her with buoys was a matter of highest priority. The

United States Lake Survey office in Detroit, charged with the responsibility of so marking any such hazardous obstruction, sent a team of sweep vessels to the scene. For two weeks they sought her, sweeping back and forth in the grids of charted courses. Finally, on April 23 they found her, a scant 800 feet from the downbound sailing course but several miles from where she had foundered!

But the stubborn *Cort,* as though she had not already caused enough trouble, was not about to be an easy salvage job. Divers and wreckers, plagued by bad weather, worked for two months patching the hole the *Midvale* had punched in her hull and making all her hatches and openings air and water tight. Nor did it matter to her that midway in the operation a court-appointed arbitrator found her at fault for backing into the path of the *Midvale.*

Late in June the wreckers judged the *Cort* to be sufficiently tight to be pumped out. Around the clock, clanking big steam pumps on the salvage vessels sucked the water from her holds and engine room. Success was practically in sight with the *Cort* showing some signs of life and movement when, with a great uproar and spouting geysers of water, her decks collapsed. Now she was in truly bad shape.

By late September the wrecking crews had completed preparations for the only alternative method of salvaging her and one they had hoped to avoid—an expensive cofferdam built completely around her. On a bright and warm Sunday she came up, battered, still seemingly defiant and surrounded by a fleet of salvage craft and pleasure-boat sightseers. After anchoring off Bar Point for temporary repairs she was dragged away to the Toledo Shipbuilding Company by the tugs *Harding, Michigan* and *Trotter.*

The shipyards were already working at capacity on new

tonnage and the repair of larger vessels, so the *Cort* was tied up to stew and sulk until after the November Armistice. When the yard men did get around to her they did a most complete job, practically rebuilding her. Her main deck was renewed and raised four feet, and her after accommodations were enlarged and modernized. She emerged a vastly changed vessel, but with no real assurance that her disposition had reverted to the model of behavior status prior to the ice fiasco. However, she soon gave every indication of having reformed, for she again performed her tasks without complaint or revolt.

Every spring the *Cort* and *Neilson,* still considered the prime icebreakers of the Pittsburgh fleet, led the first contingent of upbound vessels through the ice-jammed Detroit, St. Clair and St. Marys rivers. The *Cort*'s only show of temper was in April of 1927. While leading the way up the lower St. Marys, the *Neilson* stripped the blades or "buckets" off her propeller. Not to be outdone by her sister ship, the *Cort,* in a fit of petulance, did the same thing a few hours later. But when the detachable blades were replaced with new ones the two ships continued on to the upper St. Marys and out into Whitefish Bay, in Lake Superior, where they worked most effectively in assisting other steamers in the vicinity of Parisian Island.

But icebreakers or no, the days of 320-foot whaleback steamers were numbered. No longer able to compete with newer and larger vessels they fell upon evil days. Both the *Cort* and *Neilson* were sold to other interests whose operations could be adequately served with the smaller, specialized boats. The *Cort* was sold to the Lake Ports Shipping & Navigation Company, of Detroit, but retained her name. The *Neilson,* acquired by another firm, became the *J. T. Reid.*

The *Cort,* subject to extensive changes and conversion in Lorain, began her new career in June of 1927, her profile altered considerably by two large whirley cranes on newly installed deck rails. The little turret near the bow also vanished, replaced with a larger deck house for additional crew housing and the gear she would need in her new trade, which essentially was that of a tramp ship capable of carrying a variety of cargoes which could be unloaded or loaded by the cranes. The cranes could efficiently handle pig iron and scrap when equipped with magnets or, when the magnets were replaced by grab buckets, bulk cargoes such as coal, stone, slag or sand could be handled just as effectively.

It was now, when her former Pittsburgh Steamship Company crew no longer figured in her future, that Augie Britz began his career as the *Cort's* chief engineer, a crises-plagued alliance that was to bring adventure and grievous happenings before Augie became disenchanted with his lot in life.

From Lorain the *Cort* steamed directly for Tonawanda, New York, for what was to be the first of many cargoes of scrap or pig iron. It was a trade, though honorable, that took her into the smelly waters of mill and foundry slips, there to tie up for hours while the cranes disgorged her load. For the balance of the season she operated on a short-haul shuttle, carrying scrap iron from Detroit to the Otis Steel plant, far up the winding Cuyahoga River, in Cleveland.

It took only slightly longer than a year for the now-aging whaleback to display a flash of temper. It was as though she had been deliberately giving her new and lowly role a chance to reveal some of her redeeming qualities but had finally run out of patience. Now she exhibited the same irascible sort of tantrum that had sunk her in the gray murk of cold winter dusk of December 17, 1917. In the dark hours before dawn on August 30, 1928, while bound from Cleveland to Chicago with pig iron, she drove hard on Colchester Reef, in western Lake Erie, a scant twelve miles from the scene of her previous bit of mischief off Bar Point.

The captain of the tug *Florida,* sent to her aid, reported back that she was out six feet forward, hard on rock bottom, and that her cargo hold was flooded, although Augie Britz had quickly activated steam pumps that kept her engine room free of water. Harassed by bad weather, it took the Great Lakes Towing Company's salvage fleet, with the wrecking steamer *Favorite* and the lighters *Newman* and *Rescue,* six days to free her, and then only after 2300 tons of her pig iron had been lightered. Buckled and battered, she was towed to the Great Lakes Engineering Company, at River Rouge, Michigan, for extensive repairs.

The season of 1933 started auspiciously for the *Cort* since she had the honor of opening the navigation season at Cleveland by bringing in a cargo of scrap iron from Detroit, again hauling it up the Cuyahoga River, this time to the old Corrigan-McKinney steel plant. It proved to be a long, hard season. The whaleback, now beginning to feel the years in her bones, was one of the last vessels to lay up that year, and under distressing circumstances. Some sailors said again that it was just the frustrated personality of an old lady who deserved better things, but the cold fact is that, while downbound in the Livingston Channel of the Detroit River, on her last trip of the season, she "touched" on Ballards Reef, doing considerable bottom damage. Augie Britz, with first assistant engineer, Louis Rosie, at his side, again did yeoman duty in keeping the pumps pounding at full capacity as the tugs escorted her back to Detroit. But the water was coming in faster than it could be pumped out, and she sank as she approached the Nicholson dock. During the winter she was raised, repaired and readied for another season, her owners, strangely, still considering her the ideal vessel for their operation.

Perhaps somewhat contrite after her latest escapade the *Cort* worked steadily through most of the 1934 season, again a busy one for her although the country in general was still in the throes of the Great Depression. All spring and summer she hustled from one port to another, taking on and discharging the same old scrap cargoes, breaking up the monotony somewhat by four trips into Muskegon, Michigan, with pig iron for the Campbell, Wyant and Cannon foundry. If she still burned with resentment at her come-down from the good old days of long hauls on clean freshwater, she hid it well until the season was almost over.

On November 24 she was logged upbound in the Detroit River at 2:30 P.M., bound this time for Holland, Michigan, way over on the east coast of Lake Michigan. She arrived at her destination on the twenty-sixth, languishing there for the better part of two days while the cranes unloaded her. She departed for Chicago and another load of pig iron at 9:00 P.M. on the twenty-eighth. But Lake Michigan was in an unkindly mood and a southwesterly gale blew up, increasing in fury as the hours passed. Whalebacks were never known for their sea-kindly habits in a head wind and sea. Without a conventional stem but with their raking, spoon-shaped bows, they were extremely difficult to hold into the wind when they were without cargo. Bucking directly into the gale on her Chicago course, the *Cort* made painfully slow progress. With the weight of the two big whirley cranes topsides, Captain Charles E. Cox was reluctant to attempt a turn and run before the storm, fearing his vessel might capsize. But just off Michigan City, Indiana, the fierce wind and a towering sea did it for him, swinging the *Cort* completely around so that she was headed back to her port of departure, wallowing heavily and taking big seas over her deck.

Captain Cox later recounted that at this point he had but two alternatives, neither of them very promising or comforting: let his boat go with the wind and seas and drive her ashore on the sands at Little Point Sable, or try for the harbor at Muskegon, protected by breakwaters. He chose the latter and at ten o'clock on that wild night of November 30, came within a whisker of making it. But just as the *Cort* was making her turn to line up with the entrance piers, a huge sea created by the backwash off the breakwater meeting a big incoming comber lifted the ship like a cork and smashed her against the outside of the north breakwater, grinding out her bottom and buckling in her port side plates. There, she settled quickly, heeled to starboard at about a thirty-degree angle, parallel to the breakwater and impaled on the riprap stone that formed the sloping underwater breakwater base or foundation.

Firmly planted there, her keel already on the sand bottom, she was still 3000 feet from shore and being systematically raked by the tattered remnants of every sea that climbed over the breakwater to pummel her deck and lash at her cabins. The lights had gone out immediately and cook Harry Sutton had been knocked down and showered with dishes and pans that flew from their racks. This time even Augie Britz was powerless to stem the catastrophic flood of water that surged up into the cargo holds and engine room.

The *Cort*'s plight had been noted by the surfman on watch

at the Muskegon Coast Guard. He saw her lifted high and dashed on the rock breakwater, observed her lights flicker and go out, and knew at once that her people were in mortal peril. The alarm was sounded and chief boatswain's mate, John A. Basch, called off a crew of four and put out in the station's largest power surfboat. Dashed about like a cork and lifted precipitously on each incoming crest, the surfboat made precious little headway. At times the crests would throw the boat completely out of the water and she would drop down into the valleys with force that would have demolished an ordinary craft. A major problem was that in the pitch-black of night they could not see or judge the angle or height of the smashing seas. Still she plugged on with Basch trying to gauge the pitch of the watery inclines and thus spare the boat as much punishment as possible. As they neared the wreck the seas were even more violent. A particularly nasty one heaved the surfboat skyward with such force that when she crashed down again young surfman Jack Dipert was gone, flipped out of the boat like a pea bursting from a ruptured pod! Ironically, at that very moment, his father, William Dipert, in command of the Coast Guard station at Point Betsy, was busy watching the storm-tossed lake for other possible victims.

Boatswain's mate Basch and his crew, drenched by freezing seas and now reduced to three, fought on, taking each sea as a momentary adversary, discarding it in seconds to engage another in head-to-head combat. They had almost reached the stricken *Cort* when one truly gigantic crest flipped the boat over, dumping Basch and his men out. Even though supported by their life jackets they barely had enough strength to fight their way to the beach.

Despite the lateness of the hour the cry of "shipwreck" spread through Muskegon like wildfire. From every section of town came a stream of automobiles heading for the wind-swept beach north of town, a veritable cavalcade whose numbers swelled by the moment. The people of Muskegon, because so many of their own had been and still were closely involved in lake shipping, had a great empathy for sailors, particularly in these hard depression years. Out the scenic highway they sped, there to park their cars and dash to the beach where, even as the vanguard arrived, Basch and his luckless and exhausted crew were crawling out of the surf. Here the early arrivals were joined by the young men of the Civilian Conservation Corps, another product of the Great Depression, stationed at the barracks at Muskegon Dunes State Park. Frantically they joined the townspeople in combing the beach for the body of young Jack Dipert or any of the *Cort*'s people who might have been swept overboard. The search was fruitless.

Chief boatswain's mate Basch wasted little time in informing his superiors that more help was needed if the marooned crew of the *Cort* were to be rescued, assuming that they were still alive and sheltered in the wrecked whaleback. There had been no signal or indication of life aboard, but considering the conditions, with monster seas climbing the breakwater and smothering the vessel in spume and spray, there was little likelihood of any such signals being attempted, or of being observed had they been made.

In response to Basch's request for help both the White Lake station to the north and the Grand Haven station to the south sent their largest surfboats to the scene. The Grand Haven boat, with six men under command of chief boatswain's mate William E. Preston, made the perilous trip under the worst possible sea conditions, passing within one hundred feet of the *Cort* when making the breakwater entrance. It was impossible to attempt a rescue in total darkness but the surfboat men could see no sign of life. The Coast Guard boats rendezvoused in the protected channel and consulted with Lieutenant Ward W. Bennett, commandant of the Tenth Coast Guard District, who had driven furiously from Grand Haven to take command of the rescue effort. It was his decision, after talking to Basch and Preston, that any attempt at a hasty, impulsive rescue try in the darkness would be doomed to failure and that a coordinated effort would be made at daybreak.

It was a foregone conclusion by those on shore that the *Cort*'s crew, if indeed they were still alive, would be suffering greatly from the cold, and they would also be aware that no rescue craft could approach them before daylight. All along the shore the watchers maintained bonfires throughout the night to assure the crew that their plight was known and to please have heart and hope. Others, keeping a vigil in the long rows of cars along the scenic highway at the state park, flashed their headlights on and off as another indication that help would come. And from the elevation of the highway, watchers could see the lights of the Coast Guard cutter *Escanaba,* patrolling outside the breakwater and rolling and pitching villainously.

It would have been completely disillusioning to those worrying and praying on shore had they known the true conditions aboard the *Cort* during the long dark hours she was under assault. The first reaction of the crew, most of them knocked off their feet at the moment of impact with the breakwater, was to ignore the danger of being swept overboard in a mad rush to the forward deckhouse, fearful that the steamer's boilers might explode when the cold water surged in through the crumpled hull plates. But Augie Britz, in his last act before abandoning his post, took the necessary steps that might prevent such a calamity. Soon, when it was apparent that the boilers were not going to blow and that the *Cort* was not going to roll over, the crew crept cautiously back to the after cabins, still under siege by the crests of seas that had expended their true force against the breakwater.

Fumbling around in total darkness for some time, one man found a lantern, another some candles. Then there was enough light to take stock of their uncertain situation. Almost subconsciously they gravitated to the galley, the favorite forum of sailors whatever their plight or danger. Cook Sutton's coal range had been torn from its moorings by the force of the collision and the smoke pipe disjointed, but it was only a matter of moments and a little muscle to repair the damage and soon a brisk coal fire was burning again. In the light of the lantern and flickering candles Sutton made fresh coffee and brought out turkey left over from Thanksgiving, mince pie and fruit. More lanterns were activated and, all in all, it was quite a cozy gathering. Some crew members scrawled into their bunks to sleep while others organized a lively card game at the mess table.

At dawn, with the seas moderating, the Coast Guardsmen put their plan into effect. The Muskegon men, roped together for safety, would slowly inch their way out the 3000-foot breakwater, hopefully to a point beside the stricken vessel. Meanwhile, chief boatswain's mate Preston would take his large surfboat out along the exposed outer side of the breakwater in the event some of the Muskegon station men were swept off by the gray seas which still surged over it with some regularity. The breakwater, constructed of huge stone slabs, with no continuity or regular conformation, was difficult to walk on under the best of conditions. Now, constantly awash, it was a slippery and formidable challenge. Out the men went at a snail's pace, their progress watched breathlessly from ashore.

Preston's surfboat started out briskly enough, but was rudely buffeted and turned around by the first seas encountered outside the protected waters. But the determined Preston turned his boat and tried again, heading directly into the seas, the ensuing spray often hiding boat and crew from the sight of those who watched. Try as he might, the brave skipper of the surfboat could not get his craft out to the *Cort* and finally had to admit defeat by returning again to sheltered waters.

The Muskegon men, however, were making distinct progress and, to the accompaniment of cheers they could not hear, finally succeeded in reaching a point directly beside the *Cort's* after cabins. The stranded steamer's crew had been watching the ant-like progress of the hardy lifesavers through the portholes and were waiting, cheering and shivering on the boat deck, some distance above the breakwater. A line curled up and out, and in minutes an umbilical cord between the stricken whaleback became a manila highway to rescue. One by one the twenty-five men of the *Cort's* crew came down the line on an improvised breeches buoy, cook Harry Sutton first, followed by first mate Harvey Matthews. Both pitched in to help the others, some of whom were now suffering from fatigue and the extreme cold.

Now another ordeal lay ahead. In three groups, again lashed together like alpine climbers, they began the long, perilous trek along the wave-lashed breakwater. Although led and assisted by the Coast Guardsmen who were also tethered, some slipped and would have drowned had not the others pulled them, bruised and shaken, to safety. Near the end of the agonizing journey Harry Sutton collapsed and was carried in a blanket the rest of the way.

Eager hands were there to help once the beach was reached, but many of the half-frozen seamen were too cold to hold the steaming cups of coffee that were proffered them. Harry Sutton and mate Matthews were thought to be in a bad way and were rushed to a hospital in Muskegon. The others were led to the Civilian Conservation Corps barracks where hot food and warm, dry clothing left them little the worse for their experience.

Solemn pledges were made that day, one of them the very instant the safety of the beach was reached. It was made by shivering Augie Britz, the chief engineer, who had just suffered his third shipwreck on the boat with the deplorable and unpredictable disposition. Standing there looking back at the *Cort,* a blanket over his shaking shoulders and his face stung with blowing sand and spray, he came to a momentous decision.

"To hell with 'er!" said Augie Britz.

---

1 The *James B. Neilson,* née *Washburn,* and finally the *J. T. Reid,* also fell upon evil days in her advancing years, carrying varied cargoes, including automobiles from Detroit. In 1936, two years after her sister ship, the *Henry Cort,* impaled herself on the Muskegon breakwater, where incidentally, she still lies, the *Reid* was taken to the plant of the Interlake Engineering Company, along Cleveland's serpentine Cuyahoga River, there to be cut up for scrap.

# 9

## *A Cousin in Need Is a Cousin Indeed*

Part way up the lovely Bruce Peninsula of Ontario, flanked by Georgian Bay on the east and Lake Huron on the west, where pollution for the most part has still to raise its murky head, is the pleasant town of Wiarton. It is the largest community between Owen Sound and Tobermory, at the northernmost tip of the peninsula, and the jumping-off place for Manitoulin Island, Little Current and the Blind River country. At the head of Colpoys Bay, it is smack dab in the center of an area long frequented by discriminating tourists and "summer folk," its population consequently trebling during the season. But, coincidentally, at that very same time a considerable number of the town's stalwart citizens are notable by their absence. They depart before the seasonal influx and return long after the blue waters of the bay are devoid of water skiers, fair-weather fishermen or trim sailboats skimming over the fathoms-deep grave of the *Jane Miller*.

The absent ones have nothing against the tourists, of course, but they have their living to make, and they make it

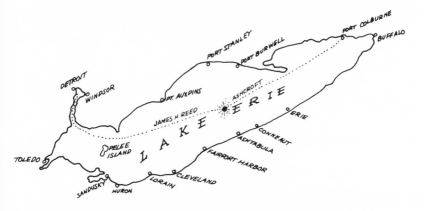

on the steamboats of the Great Lakes. Few communities have sent so many native boys to the freshwater shipping lanes and even fewer have seen so many of their own sons rise to command. At one time no less than four commodores or senior captains of major Canadian fleets called Wiarton home and hastened to embrace its warmth and friendliness when the long shipping seasons ended. Wilf Lemcke of the Misener fleet, Eric Fox of the Upper Lakes & St. Lawrence Navigation Company, Harold Miller of Canada Steamship Lines and Don Steip of the Paterson Steamship Company all began their careers in humble roles but stuck tenaciously to their goals over difficult years to finally reach the pinnacle of their demanding professions. Wiarton honors them, and they her.

In the early 1930s, as had always been the case, many young Wiarton boys were dreaming only of the day when they would be old enough to sail. Three of the dreamers were cousins, Alfred Spragge,[1] Doug Hepburn and Melvin Buckland,[2] still in school but counting the months and years until they, too, could depart with the veteran sailors. In a town the size of Wiarton, everybody knew everybody else. Experienced steamboat men, when in a position to do so, were more than likely to help a young man get his first berth aboard ship, menial though the tasks might be. Oilers, wipers, deckhands, porters and coal passers were thus often young in years but strong in ambition and determination.

In 1934, when Alfred Spragge was fifteen, his father, a marine engineer, moved his family to Ashtabula, Ohio, where young Alfred finished his schooling at the age of seventeen and promptly got a job as a fireman with the Hanna fleet, headquartered in Cleveland. It was brutally hard, dirty work, but the Great Depression was still upon the land and it was a start. Beginning his career in the dark hold, it was only natural that his interest should be like his father's, in the machinery that propelled the vessels. Perhaps the greatest inducement for advancement was the daily contact with veteran firemen, some of them three times his age and still largely a hard-drinking, impoverished and itinerate lot. Theirs was a thankless, unrewarding job. Only when one yearned for more challenging tasks did the opportunities for advancement present themselves. Always, the mental picture of the sweating fireman was a powerful incentive for a more promising future. Normal attrition in the engine room finally created an opening for an oiler, and after sufficient experience and study at the winter school of the Lake Carriers' Association, Spragge finally qualified as a third assistant engineer, still several rungs down the ladder from the top job as chief, but better, much better, than firing.

Still with the Hanna fleet when the "third's" ticket became his, Spragge, in the fall of 1943, was faced with the problem of working for a fleet with a surfeit of engineers. On the other hand, the Interlake Steamship Company, with thirty-nine active vessels, had a pressing need for men with his qualifications. Without surrendering his seniority with the Hanna organization, it was arranged that, rather than stay on as an oiler or wiper, he would join the crew of Interlake's *James H. Reed* on a sort of lend-lease basis. The working arrangement would enable him to accrue the experience and service time necessary to qualify for a second engineer's license. Starting in September, he finished the season on the *Reed*.

The same situation prevailed early in 1944, although every bottom that would float was busy carrying iron ore to feed the massive American war machine. Vessels that would have gone to the scrap pile in the 1930s had not depression prices and lack of scrap demand ruled otherwise were busy shuttling back and forth from Duluth, Two Harbors, Marquette and Escanaba to the lower-lakes mill ports with ore. But as the war lengthened the working life of vessels, so did it prolong the careers of lake officers. Captains, mates and engineers who might earlier have considered retirement kept on "doing their part" in the war effort.

So back to the *Reed,* fitting out in Toledo, went Alfred Spragge, still on lend-lease but as determined as ever to make his mark in the licensed ranks of the engine room. Like all Great Lakes vessels the *Reed* had to do its part in replenishing ore stockpiles, depleted by peak steel production during the winter. The ships started out early, perhaps too early, but time and iron ore were of the essence as the Nazi forces were still powerful, and the Japanese far from defeated in the Pacific theater.

Built in 1903, the 448-foot *Reed* was originally one of the "submarine" type vessels with a flush deck aft, and the crew's quarters and galley below the spar deck. Later, when maritime laws limited the number of hours seamen could work, thus necessitating larger crews and accommodations to house them, the *Reed* was modernized with new crew's quarters, galley and other facilities included in a new raised deck aft. Still, with many hatches, on twelve-foot centers, the *Reed*, with a cargo capacity of only 7800 tons, was an old and obsolete boat as the economics of shipping dictate. She would doubtless have made her way to the ship breakers had not World War II precluded the age consideration, thus granting her a reprieve.

The Canadian fleets were equally hard pressed for bottoms and qualified men to sail them. Creaking old vessels, laid up for long years and available only because pre-war scrap prices had delayed their being cut up, went to sea again in the service of the Dominion. Unionists on both sides of the international boundary complained frequently and loudly to authorities that many such vessels were sailing short-handed and with too few experienced men. But the exigencies of war drowned out their laments. The important thing was to move the cargoes of iron ore, coal, limestone and grain.

Alfred Spragge, now twenty-four years old and back again as third assistant engineer on the *Reed*, often wondered about his Wiarton cousins, Doug Hepburn and Melvin Buckland. He knew that both were sailing in the Canadian fleets but not on what vessels, or for what steamship lines. This he had learned from family correspondence, for the early spring fitouts and lengthened seasons, along with gasoline rationing, had prevented the usual winter visits to his boyhood haunts. The cousins, likewise, knew only that Spragge was gainfully employed on a steamboat, working up to his announced goal of chief engineer.

The *Reed* loaded her first 1944 cargo of iron ore at Duluth, the task as always supervised by the first mate, in this case Malcolm E. Moore. There was plenty of ice in Lake Superior that spring and it continued to harass the *Reed* and other vessels all the way down the St. Marys River, Lake Huron and in the St. Clair River. The weather was cold and blustery, inspiring all hands to make frequent visits to the galley, presided over by a highly competent husband-and-wife team, Ray and Camille Losey. Man and wife stewards were not unusual on Great Lakes steamboats, the employment of couples being rather common on steamers of United States registry and even more prevalent in the Canadian fleets. The policy achieved two objectives: it prevented the long seasonal separation of the pair and provided a more substantial family income. Ray and Camille Losey, who always kept a fresh urn of hot coffee, had been shipmates and helpmates for years.

In the wee hours of the morning of April 27, the *Reed* was but one of many boats slogging along in a pea-soup fog on Lake Erie, bound for Buffalo with her ore cargo. One of them was the 524-foot steamer *Ashcroft,* of the Canada Steamship Lines, with J. F. "Kid Gloves" Davis in command. Early on the previous evening the *Ashcroft* had cleared the Welland Canal at Port Colborne, bound for Toledo to pick up a coal cargo. Ice, driven by the prevailing westerly winds the length of the lakes, had accumulated as always at the eastern end of the lake. Captain Davis, setting a course that would keep him well off Long Point, proceeded cautiously for some time. The ice has been known to pile up in impressive windrows and impenetrable masses, but this time the *Ashcroft* met only drifting slush ice before working her way into clear water. The danger past except for drifting fields that might be encountered any time, Captain Davis then established an angling course for Southeast Shoal and Pelee Passage, the next trouble spot for mariners bound the length of Lake Erie. Quickly calculating distance, time and the *Ashcroft's* speed, he was happy to note that the passage would be made in daylight. It was an extremely dangerous area as the bottom was littered with the bones of meeting vessels that had not passed in the night, thus effectively contradicting the old, poetic phrase. All through the night the hooting of fog whistles on other vessels could be heard, with the *Ashcroft* adding to the mournful din with her own throaty blasts.

Aboard the *Reed,* Captain Bert Brightstone, after lingering in the pilot house until long after midnight, went below to his cabin for a bit of well-deserved sleep, leaving first mate Malcolm Moore with the standard shipboard admonition to call him should anything unusual in the way of weather or traffic develop. The *Reed,* too, was giving out with the regulation fog signals, three raucous bleats at one-minute intervals. It was not an atmosphere conducive to sleep, but Captain Brightstone, bone-weary and red-eyed from the lack of it, was not to be denied his rest. At the last reckoning he and mate Moore had agreed that their vessel was about twenty-six miles directly north of Ashtabula.

Standard Lake Erie courses, steered by generations of skippers with only magnetic compasses, would normally keep eastbound and westbound steamer traffic lanes well apart. One usually had to be alert only for vessels angling in or out of some south-shore ports such as Erie, Conneaut, Ashtabula, Fairport Harbor, Cleveland, Lorain, Huron or Sandusky. The only other contingency to be reckoned with was the carferry *Ashtabula,* which regularly crossed the steamer tracks on her voyages from Ashtabula to Port Burwell, Ontario.

Radar was still undreamed of except for a chosen few in the military, but it would have been a heaven-sent blessing on such a night. The wind was modest but did nothing to dispel the fog, although it did build up short, choppy seas, the kind sailors describe as "a nasty bit of slop." Silently, except for the straggling chorus of distant, raspy whistles, the usual armada of commercial vessels went about their business, each plodding along on her personal rendezvous with a distant dock. The water temperature was forty-two degrees.

Aboard the *Reed* at 5:00 A.M. on that morning of April 27, the around-the-clock routine of shipboard life found only those on duty awake and duly attending to their chores. Mike Obester, second assistant engineer, was at his post near the engine controls. An oiler was going about the designated agenda of his lubricating schedule. In the black hold the firemen and coal passers were making all the banging and clanging noises associated with such strenuous work. Third assistant engineer Alfred Spragge, relieved by first assistant Arnold Kienitz at 10:00 P.M., dallied briefly in the galley before going to the room he shared with second assistant Obester. The two chatted for a few minutes before Spragge dropped off to sleep. Obester was due to go on watch at 4:00 A.M.

Forward, in the darkness of the pilot house, wheelsman Fred Preston was silent and watchful as first mate Moore paced back and forth. Despite the decidedly cool temperature several windows were open to permit the sounds of the distant whistles to be heard and their proximity judged. But now mate Moore was concerned and apprehensive. There was a single, persistent whistle which in his judgment seemed to be growing louder with each sounding of the prescribed three hoots. Ever mindful of the master's orders to awaken him should danger or unusual circumstances transpire, he bounded down the companionway to pound on Captain Brightstone's door. "There seems to be another vessel nearby," he called.

Captain Brightstone, who had merely reclined without getting undressed, was out the door and on his way to the pilot house in seconds. He, too, with that unerring instinct that smelled danger, thought the whistle was uncomfortably close. It was 5:04 A.M.

"Get the men up and out," he ordered mate Moore. At the same time he swung the telegraph indicator to "stop" and grabbed the whistle pull, giving a series of short blasts, the danger signal. Again came a seemingly mocking answer as an unseen vessel made her presence known somewhere out there in the fog. But again the sound was nearer and ominously louder. Waiting not a second longer, Captain Brightstone closed the knife switch on the general alarm. At almost the same instant the lights of the other vessel loomed up on the port side, bearing down on what was obviously a collision course! Both the captain and wheelsman Preston grabbed life preservers and bolted out the door and started down the companionway. At this precise instant the stranger, without cargo and riding high, plowed into the *Reed,* cutting nearly halfway through her hull, at about number-eight hatch. It was exactly 5:08 A.M.!

So quickly did the tremendous inrush of water overwhelm the ore-laden *Reed* that she started to founder immediately. Indeed, Captain Brightstone and wheelsman Preston, still on the companionway between the pilot house and Texas deck, were smashed against the bulkhead by the frigid, engulfing seas, tangled momentarily in a welter of lines and wreckage. But they kicked their way free and floated together until they managed to grasp the small life raft that had been on the roof of the pilot house.

Mate Moore had done his best to rouse all the forward crew, screaming and pounding on doors until the sleepy-eyed occupants began streaming out, ill-clad for such an early-morning outing. All got out and on deck, apparently, except second mate Martin Mattson. Third mate John I. Cummings,[3] who shared a room with him, recalled later that Mattson got up, fumbled for some clothing and was, he thought, right behind him. But mate Cummings was seconds ahead of the rush of water that trapped the captain and wheelsman and he managed to reach the boat deck where some of the after-end crew were already ripping the canvas covers off the boats.

With the single exception of mate Mattson the forward crew all reached the spar deck and began a perilous dash aft to the lifeboats. Down the deck they ran, most of them barefooted, dashing through a cloud of roaring steam from broken heating and machinery piping. Hatches were exploding upward from the compression of air in the holds, and the cold water was already lapping at their feet. Back they ran, often stumbling over wreckage. Wheelsmen Joseph Zeigler and Clinton Meyers pelted along in the cold and dark with deckhands Marlon Godshalk, John Laucka, Wilbert Tayra, Doyle Rogers and Eugene Lockwood. With them were watchmen George Moesinger, Reuben White, Abraham Guberski and George Miller, all desperate men on a frightful journey. The high bow of the other vessel loomed over them, and to add to the nightmarish scene, her whistle, still set for the automatic sounding of the fog signal, continued its ear-splitting blasts.

The group they joined aft were in a similar state of frantic haste. Engineer on watch, Arnold Kienitz, had alerted chief Engineer Robert O. Fletcher by a room-bell signal as soon as the engine was ordered reversed. Fletcher could already hear the general alarm ringing and yelled to the engine room and fire-hold men to abandon their posts. They, he and Kienitz, pausing only long enough to get life preservers from their rooms, ran down the hallways, pounding on doors and shouting for everybody to get up and out on deck. But here, too, there was one man who apparently failed to hear and either slept on or was slow to respond, coal passer George Statkis.

Deckhand Marlon Godshalk saw Ray and Camille Losey emerge from their cabin and pause on the lower deck. Mrs. Losey, in her nightgown and robe, was clutching the rail, crying and obviously almost paralyzed with fear. Her husband was urging her to go topsides to the boats but she clung there in stark terror, refusing with mute shakings of her head.

Alfred Spragge heard the alarm bell and the chief's shouted orders to get out but still had no inkling of what had happened. He had felt the jar as the other vessel's stem ripped into the *Reed*'s port side but the jolt was so slight he assumed that the *Reed* had merely encountered a field of ice. But he, too, joined the mad rush topsides where the earlier arrivals such as oilers William Nappi and James Koren were trying frantically to launch the boats. The canvas covers were already off, but the hand-cranked davits were slow in responding to efforts to swing them out. In the darkness men bumped into each other, fell down and rose to batter the boats with their shoulders, trying to hasten the action of the davits.

From beneath them there were vast rumblings and great noises from the boiler room as cold water hit hot metal. A final tremendous, thunder-like explosion from below sent a Vesuvius of fire, steam and hot coals up through the funnel, the smoking debris dropping down upon the desperate men trying vainly to launch the boats. The *Reed* was going down fast. It was obvious that she would take her plunge before the davits could be cranked out.

"There's no time . . . no time," shouted chief engineer Fletcher. "Just unhook them and they'll float free." The advice came too late.

"Then she just slid down from under us," recalls Spragge. "We were all in the water, the cold just took your breath away."

Chief engineer Fletcher, now retired, remembers the moment with painful clarity. "She just went down like a rock," says Fletcher.

Deckhand Marlon Godshalk's last vision as the *Reed* headed for the bottom was of the Loseys, still huddled at the rail, with Ray's arms around his wife. "She couldn't swim and was afraid to go overboard," said Godshalk. "His arms were around her as they drowned."

Great grouts of water and steam spurted upward as the *Reed* sought her final port, spewing all sorts of wreckage amid those thrashing around in the frigid water. And at this time the crews of both vessels were still unaware of the identity of the other steamer.

Some died quickly, either of drowning or exposure—watchmen George Miller and Abraham Guberski, fireman George Grignon and the devoted pair from the galley, Ray and Camille Losey. Second mate Mattson and coal passer George Statkis were already gone.

Captain Brightstone and wheelsman Preston still had their little white life raft. Others grabbed whatever they could find that would support them. Third mate Cummings heard and felt the *Reed* hit bottom as he was thrown against something solid and upright by the upward surge of water. He grabbed whatever it was and held on. It was some time before he became aware that it was the vessel's after spar or mast and it became his personal refuge until he was rescued.

Most of the men tried to swim merely to try to keep warm. For some it was a vain effort as the water temperature sapped their strength quickly. Soon it was all over for Spragge's roommate, Mike Obester, wheelsman Clinton Meyers, watchman Clarence Moesinger, oiler David Roberts and fireman Leonard Wisniewski. Others fought tenaciously for life, clinging to planks and life preservers. The searchlight from the other vessel played over the scene, and those in the water could hear much shouting, noises and the creaking of davits as the lifeboats were being lowered. Some in the water were afraid they couldn't last long enough to be picked up.

Aboard the *Ashcroft,* for it was indeed she who had cut the *Reed* down, Captain Davis had quickly and efficiently ordered his boats lowered and the general alarm had brought up all hands to man them. Seconds after the collision, when it was apparent the vessel he had struck was going to sink, and sink almost at once, he had ordered his wireless man to call for assistance, giving the approximate location of the mishap. In minutes the steamers *John Sherwin, Clarence B. Randall* and *Sinaloa* turned from their courses to converge on the given location. The Coast Guard cutter *Crocus* also quickly departed her moorings and headed for the scene.

Alfred Spragge found a plank to grasp and was almost immediately joined by watchman Wilbert Tayra and porter Don Reynolds. They could hear others of the *Reed*'s crew shouting and floundering around nearby and see a significant showing of portable lights as the *Ashcroft*'s boats hit the water.

The *Ashcroft*'s second mate was in charge of one of the lifeboats which pulled briskly toward the desperate sounds in the night as those in the water yelled frantically for assistance lest they be bypassed in the dark. The *Ashcroft,* with her bow plates and frames buckled in, still kept her big searchlight darting over the choppy waters.

Engineer Spragge saw the vague, dark silhouette of a lifeboat looming over him and the form of a man leaning over the side to help him. One hand grasped the shoulder strap of his life preserver, the other turned a flashlight on his face. "My God," the rescuer cried out, "it's my cousin!"

It was good old Melvin Buckland from back home in Wiarton!

---

1 Alfred Spragge, two weeks after the collision, was back at work on another vessel of the Interlake fleet, the steamer *John Sherwin*. He finally achieved his goal of becoming a chief engineer, back in the Hanna fleet and on the steamer *Carle C. Conway*.

2 Melvin Buckland chose to become a deck officer and, working his way upward, became second mate of the *Ashcroft*. Later, he became the highly respected skipper of Canada Steamship Line's big *Black Bay*.

3 Nor was the *Reed*'s third mate, John I. Cummings, deterred by adversity. He was sailing again in a matter of days and eventually commanded a prestige vessel in the Interlake Steamship fleet.

# 10

## "*A Toasht to the Brave Lifesh . . . er, Lifeshavers*"

**W**ESTWARD FROM THE DESOLATE hook of Long Point where the wreck-studded sands jut out into Lake Erie like the beckoning arm of doomsday, it is doubtful if any coast has claimed as many sailing craft over a relatively short span of years as the sixty-odd miles along the Ontario shore between Clear Creek and Point aux Pins. Swinging invitingly northward in a gentle crescent, as if coaxing mariners in from waters harassed by a long sweep of northerly wind, it presented, as it does today, a tempting prospect of calm seas in the lee of the shore and visions of a pleasant land rimmed by forests of chestnut and oak. But all too frequently a sudden and violent shifting of the wind to southwest or even to southeast, a trait for which Lake Erie is infamous, would quickly transform those benign waters into a death trap from which there was no escape. Too late then, a now-hostile shore almost upon them, shipmasters found themselves without sea room to make the most effective use of their canvas in clawing away from the land. Seas that developed stature quickly offered a very real threat of broaching-to, or capsizing, if an attempt was made to haul around into the wind. Inevitably, many vesels were thus lost, but, strangely, the greatest danger was not the punishing seas, the wind or lurking sandbars, but the land itself. Exceedingly fair to the eyes of the sailor when viewed from afar, it was, in reality, a coastline of disaster.

Eastward from near Point aux Pins, rising slowly but steadily, the north shoreline abandons the low and sandy, often marsh profile characteristic of western Lake Erie. Instead, as one skirts the shore eastward, the sandy beach and marsh give way to bluffs, modest at first but gaining in stature as the miles go on. Undulating occasionally and broken sharply only where streams intersect the coast, they grow in height until, for a considerable number of miles, they tower a hundred or more feet above the lake, sharp and forbidding with the seas swirling and lashing at their feet. This is the long and treacherous shore known as the "clay banks." Woe betide the sailors whose vessel came afoul the close-in sandbars. Ships and men were often hammered to death in the pounding and confused surf that often charged halfway up the bluffs. There was no escape and seldom rescue. The high bluffs continue almost to Long Point, immediately west of which they are succeeded by lower bluffs and finally by beaches and miniature sand mountains called the Houghton Sand Hills.

In truth the term "clay banks" is somewhat of a misnomer, for the bleak and precipitous walls climbing from the very surf are, often as not, yellow or red sand. But here and there, such as at Plum Point, they are indeed of clay, and doubtless some early mariner's misadventure at such a point led to the terminology. Nevertheless, as the years passed and before sail gave way to steam, those who officially recorded the comings and goings of sailing vessels, from their launchings to their demise, used an all-too-frequent five-word phrase to mark their final accounting: "Lost on the clay banks."

Along the dreaded coast there are only two ports of major significance. These were especially important in the era of sail for the receiving and shipping of coal, pig iron, fruit, general merchandise and lumber and later as terminals for railroad carferries. Twelve miles west of the site of the "old cut" at Long Point is Port Burwell. Almost the same distance farther west is Port Stanley, where Kettle Creek, meandering through much of the tobacco lands of Elgin County, makes its rendezvous with Lake Erie.

Both ports, with only modest piers extending out from the harbors, were difficult to "make" in sailing craft, except under the most salubrious and favorable wind conditions, and both supported steam tugs for assistance when needed and signaled for by a vessel captain. Even so, the passage through the piers was narrow, and when the winds were adverse big schooners were often compelled to anchor outside, "waiting for weather."

With both Port Burwell and Port Stanley exceedingly active, a goodly number of vessels came to grief on the clay banks. Trying to reach the ports by working up to them close-in to the shore, the ships were often trapped on the offshore sandbars by sudden adverse winds, or driven over them under the bluffs.

Many early wrecks went unrecorded, but the long list of vessels lost on the clay banks and so noted by history begins in 1848 when the schooner *Scotland* went ashore, a complete wreck, at Port Stanley, and the *Martha Freeme* piled on and was demolished at Port Burwell. Natives were still salvaging the iron from the *Scotland* wreck when the *Ottawa* stranded and went to pieces just west of the harbor. In 1854 the bark *Globe* "went on" at Port Burwell, and the brig *Burlington* came to grief at Port Bruce, a smaller port midway between Port Stanley and Port Burwell. Two brigs, the *Josephine* and the *Baltin,* were lost the next year, one near each of the larger ports. The bluffs at Port Burwell gathered in three more schooners in the next three years, the *Robert Bruce,* the *Everett* and the *J. A. Hope.* The schooner *Constitution* was trapped under the bluffs near Port Bruce and shredded by the seas in 1859.

The first steamer to fall victim to the clay banks was the *Bay City,* in 1862, the same year the bark *Northern Light* pounded ashore at Port Burwell and the schooner *Excelsior* was lost at Port Stanley. The trim schooner *Crevola* came to a sad end at Port Bruce in 1863, the same year the *George Davis* pounded herself to pieces against the bluffs at Port Burwell. After a season without serious mishap the schooner *Frontenac* "took the ground" at Port Burwell, followed the next year by a similar craft called *Tom Wrong.* The schooner *F. L. Wells,* her canvas in shreds, came romping in to her doom at Port Bruce in 1868, her wreckage lacing the foot of the bluffs for miles. At Port Burwell the clay banks and the billowing surf at their feet gathered in the schooners *Leviathan* in 1870 and the *George M. Abell* the next year.

Little wonder then, after viewing the statistics, that when Canadian authorities established lifesaving stations on the Great Lakes, the first one on Lake Erie was activated in 1885, at Port Stanley. William Berry was named coxswain. The lifeboat, self-righting and self-bailing, was manned by four regular men, including Berry who, when the alarm sounded, traditionally requested volunteer oarsmen from the local citizens.

Unaccountably, the next four years were quiet ones along the clay banks. Coxswain Berry and his crew conducted regular drills but rendered only routine service to vessels temporarily aground, and to yachtsmen who blundered onto the sandbars. They were too far away to be of help to the disaster-plagued Canadian schooner *Erie Wave* which came yawing noisily ashore in 1889. Captain Stafford had successfully clawed away from the clay banks in a brawling southwesterly gale only to go hard ashore in the shelving sand near the Houghton Sand Hills. After being stranded for several days and unsuccessful in his initial efforts to free his vessel, he had recruited an extra crew to assist in the salvage. They had freed her from the sand and were kedging her off into deeper water when one of Lake Erie's furious and sudden squalls swept in and capsized the schooner, drowning eight of the ten men aboard. Strangely, this was the third time in her unlucky career that the *Erie Wave* had capsized, on each occasion drowning some of her crew or passengers.

Two years later the Port Stanley lifeboat and its crew performed nobly in their first real challenge. On November 19, 1891, the schooner *E. G. Benedict* came storming in with a following sea, missed the piers and broached-to, foundering practically in the harbor. The crew of six, taking to the rigging as the *Benedict* went down, were in a perilous position for some time as the frigid seas continually broke over them. Nearly dead from exposure, they were plucked from their hazardous perches by Coxswain Berry and his men, three of the lifeboat crew being volunteers. As a reward for their ser-

vices above and beyond the call of duty, the *Benedict*'s mag-
nanimous owners presented each of the lifesavers with the
princely sum of five dollars.

Over the years Captain William "Thunderation Bill" Ziem
had developed a healthy respect for Lake Erie in general, the
clay banks in particular. The weathered, surf-lashed bones
of their victims were too frequently observed to be long out
of memory for the concerned shipmaster however many times
his duties took him to the north-shore ports. The wrecks
were haunting reminders and therefore factors, conscious or
subconscious, in making the decisions all shipmasters had to
make when their orders specified Port Stanley or Port Burwell as a destination. They were always conscious of the fact
that even when they were bound elsewhere, severe and unexpected weather situations might compel them to seek refuge in either port.

A mild-mannered, sober and industrious mariner, "Thunderation Bill" Ziem had earned his colorful nickname, known
all over the lakes, simply because for him it was the ultimate
oath, the supreme expressing of contempt, anger, fear, scorn
or surprise. And Thunderation Bill had no intention of sailing anywhere near the clay banks when he piloted the
schooner *Mineral State* out of Cleveland one evening in the
fall of 1902. Indeed, he envisioned a rather routine voyage
directly across the lake to Rondeau Harbor where the loop-
ing arm of Point aux Pins offered splendid protection for the
harbor, freight docks and fishing fleet of the little village of
Erieau. The *Mineral State* had spent several days unloading
a lumber cargo at Cleveland, and another day and a half
taking on and trimming 620 tons of coal destined for the
locomotives of the L.E. & D.R.R., at Erieau. It was a rare

opportunity to secure a paying cargo for a short voyage before returning to the schooner's home port of Alpena for another lumber cargo.

The *Mineral State* was a small, Detroit-built, three-masted schooner, 137 feet of keel, and had been relatively free of accidents for all of her twenty-nine years. Captain Ziem, a strict teetotaler himself, was one-third owner of the craft, and he had quickly acquiesced when the coal cargo had been offered, knowing that the other two owners, W. H. Sanborn and F. R. Reibenach, both of Alpena, would be delighted at the prospect of earning a few extra dollars with only a minor deviation from the normal homeward course.

The wind as the *Mineral State* left Cleveland, and duly noted in the log, was light and blowing south by southwest. The barometer, Captain Ziem was pleased to observe, was high, indicating continuing southerly winds. He set the course for about due north for a time and then altered a few degrees to the east, figuring to fetch Point Talbot about daylight, at which time he figured to come about on an easy port tack to make a fair and easy entrance to Rondeau Harbor with quartering winds and seas. The barometer had indeed forecast southerly winds and southerly they were, but as the night wore on they increased to gale force.

At dawn, off Point Talbot where the captain had intended to come about and reshape his course to Rondeau, the seas had gained such stature that coming about was out of the question. The 620 tons of coal was a considerable burden for the *Mineral State,* putting her down until she had a minimum of freeboard. A port tack would necessarily have put the schooner in the trough of the seas for a time, no matter how smartly the crew handled her canvas. This, Captain Ziem knew, might be the end of her. Reluctantly then, he had to ease her on an easterly course, although the seas still piled aboard over the starboard rail with regularity.

"Thunderation," he complained to mate George Hazelwood. "We'll have to try for Port Stanley although I'm darned if I know a harder port to make in any kind of wind. But, I guess we have no choice."

They were rather close, the six men who sailed the *Mineral State,* an odd paradox to the usual crew in the waning era of the wind ships when, beyond the captain and mate, the others were often itinerants, working only long enough to accumulate a little drinkin' money before hitting the beach. Demon rum ruled the fo'c'sle, and most of those there quartered were his devoted subjects.

Thunderation Bill Ziem fancied a steadier breed of sailor and selected them carefully, consistently equating sobriety with the qualities of steadfastness and dependability he sought. To those he took aboard as part of the schooner's "family" he was a friend, father confessor, teacher, banker and financial adviser. And the crewmen enjoyed these rare benefits so long as they brought no liquor aboard and were inclined to follow his golden-rule philosophies and steadfastly eschewed the temptations ashore. To steer a wandering course back to the vessel after a shoreside excursion was to invite a stern lecture from Thunderation Bill on the abominations of strong drink and the morals of those who dispensed or consumed it. In the long run then, he ended up with a crew head and shoulders above the average. Mate Hazelwood, seaman Fred Doar and cook Fred Lecuyer were all home-town boys from Alpena. Seaman Lawrence Walther was from Bay City and William Hendrickson, the other seaman, was from Cleveland. All had been with the *Mineral State* for at least two years, this in itself a remarkable statistic, and Fred Lecuyer had been boss of the galley for three years. Food was good and plentiful and, all in all, it was a happy, competent crew, exactly the kind Thunderation Bill Ziem liked to have aboard any vessel he commanded.

Both mate Hazelwood and the captain had cheerfully predicted to each other that the seas would moderate as the morning wore on, but instead the wind increased to what they estimated as forty-five miles per hour. The seas grew even more boisterous, and dark tattered shards of clouds dipped low, seemingly desirous of uniting with the water. Off Port Stanley Captain Ziem concluded that it would be foolhardy to attempt to enter the harbor under existing conditions. The tug *Gordon Brown,* he knew, would be standing by as always with steam up and a lively crew aboard. But even with a short hawser snubbed up to hold the schooner's bows off the piers, the tug could do nothing to prevent the seas from banging the stern against the opposite pier of an altogether too-narrow-entrance channel. It was an exasperating situation and Captain Ziem permitted himself his strongest oath: "Thunderation!"

The decision to anchor until the weather moderated was made with the unanimous approval of mate Hazelwood, who hurried forward to supervise the release of the port anchor. Captain Ziem directed the lowering of the modest bit of canvas the *Mineral State* had exposed to the wind. But scarcely had the schooner swung around on her chain to head-to into the seas some two miles off the piers when the wind increased in sudden fury and veered even further to the southwest. Now virtually every sea climbed aboard over the bow, sluicing down the deck and sending spray nearly to the mast top when they met hatch coamings, cabins and solid deck fixtures. In less than five minutes much of the deck gear, fire buckets, dunnage and spare cordage had been washed overboard. Cook Lecuyer had confidently expected to prepare lunch as soon as the schooner had swung about on her anchor chain, but the seas quickly plucked out the galley window, flooded out the stove and carried away the stovepipe. Lecuyer and seaman Fred Doar also noted that the hatches were under assault and were obviously leaking badly, a fact they reported immediately to the captain.

"Thunderation!" the commander shouted. "Let's get the pumps started at once."

But even with the small donkey boiler fired up and both the hand and steam pumps working at capacity the water gained nearly three inches every fifteen minutes. A sounding showed four and one-half feet of water in the hold, fore and aft. Soon it became impossible for the crew to work on the deck, either to work the pumps or make temporary hatch-cover repairs.

In desperation the captain ordered the anchor chain slipped and two jib sails raised to bring the schooner's head around.

"Thunderation," he said angrily to mate Hazelwood. "We're going to go on the beach, but all we can do at this moment is to hope we can get her beyond the bluffs and on some sort of shelving beach."

Ironically, the only shelving beach within miles was immediately adjacent to the Port Stanley east pier, and there was no chance whatsoever of beaching the schooner there with the wind, seas and jib sails driving her eastward and even closer to the waiting clay banks. Captain Ziem had chosen the only course of action which, in this perilous moment, might save the lives of his crew. He had already resigned himself to losing his boat. Only a couple of moments after the jib sails had been raised, before they could help bring the *Mineral State*'s bow around, they surrendered to the gale, exploding in a lather of shredded, flapping canvas. In seconds the schooner was dropping ponderously into the troughs of succeeding seas, each one carrying her closer to the one-hundred-foot bluffs that featured the shoreline topography east of Port Stanley. Even from afar the crew could see the tremendous seas flinging themselves nearly halfway up the bluff. A half-hour after slipping the anchor chain the schooner struck the offshore sandbar, swinging around at an angle that left her bow deeply imbedded while the stern swung over the bar, lifting and pounding on the bottom with every sea.

Thunderation Bill Ziem, almost automatically, consulted his big pocket watch. It was high noon.

The tremendous jolts as the stern continued to pound soon broke the schooner's back, her starboard bulwarks being swept away by a single sea. The captain and crew, at first clustered in the mizzen-mast rigging, hastily abandoned their perches since it was evident that the mizzen would go quickly. Slowly, each man helping the other, they found refuge in the shrouds and gear that were part of the main mast rigging. From here they watched the mizzen topple, pulling away what was left of the after cabin. It also soon became apparent that the main mast was not long for this world. It creaked, groaned and leaned more precariously with every sea, the shrouds and lines alternately falling slack or snapping bar tight. Once more the six cold and drenched mariners worked their way forward, some trusting to the foremast shrouds, others huddling in whatever lee the modest fo'c'sle offered and hanging on to whatever felt secure for the moment. They were shaking with the cold, teeth chattering uncontrollably.

The main mast fell with a roar at three o'clock, bringing shouts of horror from what was by now a large crowd of en-thralled landlubbers gathered at the top of the bluffs a mile east of the Port Stanley piers, watching that most awesome of sights, a shipwreck! They had come from near and far, summoned by the hue and cry raised when the *Mineral State* "went on" at noon. School classes had been quickly dismissed, all stores had closed and practically the entire population of Port Stanley made the thrilling pilgrimage to the wind-swept bluffs. Although it looked to be a mad, foolhardy journey, calm and reasoning men had come prepared with ropes to lower over the bluffs just in case some of the schooner's crew might be desperate enough to try swimming in through the surging debris-laden seas.

Captain Ziem had already concluded that the lifesavers would eventually be on the scene, but he harbored some reservations about their ability to weather the seas, now put-ting on quite a spectacular show as they assaulted the Port Stanley piers. Outside the piers they charged on like uncon-trolled legions of looting bandits, eager to sack what little remained of the *Mineral State*. The question in Thundera-tion Bill's mind was whether his vessel would last much longer before disintegrating completely. Large sections of her once-sturdy hull were being plucked away, standing on end momentarily as the last of the iron bolts resisted, then wrench-ing free in seething waters black from the schooner's sea-

pillaged coal cargo. On each such occasion loud cries of
anguish and horror came from the growing crowd on the
bluffs. Soon there would be nothing for the crew to cling to.

Mate Hazelwood, shivering and jerking with the cold, was
firmly convinced that any rescue attempt the lifesavers might
mount would be a matter of too little, too late. To him the
thundering maelstrom of white water and the grinding
wreckage of the schooner at the base of the clay banks presented an option slightly more conducive to life than staying
with the wreck, now awash and flattening out with every sea
that came romping down upon them. He had been considering making a try for it since one o'clock when the mizzen
mast had toppled in a great lather of flailing lines, shrouds
and cordage. But Captain Ziem had been most adamant and
persuasive. "Thunderation, man, you'd be pounded into
jelly!"

But after the main mast crashed into the sea, the mate became insistent and Captain Ziem reluctantly agreed. It was
obvious that mate Hazelwood was suffering greatly from the
cold and might perish in any event. All but one of the
schooner's life preservers had been lost overboard earlier in
the day, but the captain strapped the remaining one on the
quivering first officer amid a flurry of Thunderations and
Godspeeds. One of the hatch covers was secured with a rope
and tossed over the starboard or lee side. Thereby, it was
decided, if the mate reached shore and was miraculously
plucked from the surf, the line would be available to others.
If he failed, he and the hatch cover could be drawn back to
the wreck. A raised arm was the agreed-upon signal should
he find the surf and wreckage too formidable and wished to
be pulled back.

With only a deck broom for a combination paddle and tiller, mate Hazelwood thrust himself upon the mercy of the seas. High on the bluffs the onlookers had already perceived the drama about to unfold and had lowered a series of stout ropes should the brave mate find himself in a position to grasp one of them. But one of the first seas encountered once he was away from the lee of the wreck turned the hatch cover upside down. Mate Hazelwood disappeared for only a few seconds and was then seen to be swimming toward the bluffs. From the wreck Captain Ziem and his men then witnessed one of the miracles they had been praying for. They saw the mate borne on the crest of a gigantic sea nearly halfway up the bluff precisely where one of the ropes was dangling. They saw him grab the rope and wrap it around his waist even as the succeeding crests alternately pounded him against and sucked him away from the rough wall of the bluff. From the wreck, momentarily unmindful of their own perilous position, they saw him drawn to the top, twisting, turning, bumping and obviously suffering every inch of the way.

"Thunderation!" howled Captain Ziem. "Thunderation."

Meanwhile, mate Hazelwood, immediately bundled into blankets and carried to the shelter of a wagon, was handed a bottle of whisky which he instantly put to the use intended. True to the discipline of a responsible vessel officer and the accepted tradition of the sea, he tearfully urged those assembled to "do something for the other boys."

Something was already being done for the other boys, although the earlier sound of the loud alarm horn at the lifesaving station had been carried inland rather than out on the lake where it would have brought hope to the utterly discouraged Captain Ziem and his men. It was now nearing five o'clock and dusk was fast approaching as the lifesaving boat was launched and prepared for whatever was to come in those punishing and confused "short" seas resulting from the backwash from the piers and the incoming combers. There was barely a boat length between crests.

Successor to William Berry, coxswain of Port Stanley's first lifesaving crew, was Captain J. Reginald Moore, a stalwart, fair-haired young man of considerable seafaring experience, but relatively new to the official government service. A quick look at the ragged combers climbing over the harbor piers had already convinced Captain Moore of the folly of taking the lifeboat out unassisted and wasting valuable minutes, perhaps hours, trying to breast the seas for a sufficient distance before turning eastward to come down on the wreck at a favorable angle. He had immediately enlisted the aid of Captain Alex Brown of the harbor tug *Gordon Brown* to tow the lifeboat well beyond the pier entrance and as close to the wreck as possible before casting the boat off. But still there was the matter of volunteers from the townsmen to fill out the crew. Moore knew them all and could pick those most likely, from long experience as fishermen, to render yeoman duty. With the captain himself at the tiller, there were three other regular members of the crew, stroke oarsman William Hough and seamen Henry Cherry and Frank Eveland.[1] Three more skilled oarsmen would be required and Captain Moore, as was tradition, called loudly for volunteers to the hundred or so who had quickly gathered. Some of them, including Alonzo Taylor, had surrendered choice vantage points on the bluffs to make their services available to the young lifeboat skipper. Captain Moore selected Taylor, Fred Pollock and Thomas Hough. Many had stepped forward when Moore had made his request, but those not chosen, now free to follow their own pursuits, quickly made their way back to the bluffs to observe the rescue attempt.

Moments before the lifeboat was launched two burlap bags were placed aboard, each containing several carefully padded bottles of whisky, donated by the local hotel. Call it custom, tradition or whatever, it is a known fact, proved over the centuries under similar circumstances, that nothing more effectively revives a man whose life signs are close to vanishing through cold and exposure than whisky. In crucial moments, when the will to live falters between surrender and one last, almost superhuman effort, whisky can mean the difference between life and death. There was some speculation among the lifesavers, and even those watching from the wind-swept bluff, that perhaps those still aboard the stranded and smashed schooner were too far gone to be aided by either the lifesavers or their precious cargo of Canada's finest.

Alex Brown, skipper of the tug, knew that the going would be rough and had his vessel buttoned up as tightly as possible, the working-deck watertight doors dogged down. Behind her, on a short hawser, came the lifeboat, her crew ready with the oars, although they would be superfluous until the tug cast them free. The *Gordon Brown* dug her nose into the rollicking seas beyond the piers, threw water high over her stack and pounded noisily down on the rising flank of the next sea. For what seemed like an eternity the tug was cuffed about as she held her head into the angling seas, snorting and puffing, her deck continually awash. Behind her the lifeboat took a similar buffeting, climbing the crest and dropping down between them with a pounding that could be heard ashore.

Bailing briskly, the crew kept their craft relatively free of heavy accumulations of water while Captain Moore, at the tiller, kept the bow in line with the tug which absorbed the brunt of the pitching and pounding. A scant quarter-mile beyond the piers the tug's skipper considered it safe to haul slowly to port, there to be helped eastward to the stricken schooner by quartering seas. Now both the tug and lifeboat were alternately rising with the crests instead of butting into them, falling off between the seas and rolling drunkenly although under control. To those watching from the harbor the lifeboat was often lost from sight as she wallowed deep in the troughs between the seas. Abreast of the wreck, now almost completely awash, the tug cast off the line, and the willing oarsmen, with William Hough counting out the stroke and shouting encouragement, pulled away and maneuvered their lifeboat into the lee of the wreck. The tug turned laboriously, put her head into the wind and hove-to, awaiting developments.

The sailors were still there, waiting in the advancing gloom of dusk, numb, despairing and exhausted, clinging with hands that had little feeling to whatever solid object they could find. Each sea now swept over them shoulder high. At one time or another during the waning hours of light, Lecuyer, Doar, Walther and Hendrickson had expressed a feeling of hopelessness and had favored taking mate Hazelwood's hazardous route in through the surf to take their chances with rescue ropes lowered from the bluffs. But Captain Ziem had been firm and his reasoning sound. He knew that the mate's rescue was little short of a miracle and that his being swept in to within an arm's length of the dangling rope was an element of luck they could not depend upon. Steadfastly he cajoled and encouraged them, insisting that the lifeboat would be along at any moment.

"Thunderation, boys," he pleaded, "let's not give up now. Think of that fine hot meal we're going to have ashore before we're much older."

Despite the flicker of hope he inspired from time to time the captain himself was convinced that the lifesavers would have a most difficult time of it, if, indeed, they were able to get out of the harbor. Nor could he discern anywhere on the bluffs, or among the hundreds gathered there, any sort of signal that help was on the way. The scene reminded him, in many ways, of the lithographs he had seen of morbid crowds gathered safely on shore while out at sea gallant ships and their crews were perishing at the hands of man's oldest enemy.

But the black smoke pouring from the tug's funnel, although quickly torn away and blown back into the town, was visual and heartening evidence that something was at last being done in their behalf. When the tug breasted the entrance and began her climbs to the crests of the seas, the sight of the little lifeboat following her brought cheer to the drenched and forlorn men of the *Mineral State.* By now they were in a sorry way, wracked with chills, shivering violently and almost overcome with the dreadful lassitude brought on by prolonged exposure and hopelessness.

"Thunderation," Captain Ziem exhorted them. "Didn't I tell you we'd be ashore for dinner? Come on, we've got to stay alive."

Aroused once more they began to pound each other to maintain some vestige of circulation in their veins. It was almost a macabre affair since they were also required to hang on to some part of the wreckage to prevent being swept overboard. Thus, with only one arm available, they flailed away at each other with what remaining strength they could muster.

With consummate skill, as stroke oarsman Hough bellowed his count, Captain Moore, avoiding fatal contact with the wreck, brought the lifeboat within six feet of where the drenched crewman clung in a human knot of survival. Captain Moore motioned them to jump, but such a course was automatic and they needed no encouragement or direction. One by one, Captain Ziem last, they jumped, landing in the boat on numbed limbs to collapse on the bottom or to be guided there by their rescuers.

Sensing that the men of the *Mineral State* were in sad shape, Captain Moore nodded to his men and the whisky bottles were instantly produced and as quickly raised to tremulous and quivering lips. The boatmen smiled and urged them to consume the contents of the life-giving elixir in goodly dollops. It was good whisky, strong, vibrant and productive of a warm, burning sensation, an utter contrast to those hopeless, chilling hours when they had clung to what was left of the schooner while the wind, seas and cold sought to rob them of life.

Captain Ziem, despite any previous compunctions he may have harbored against ardent spirits, hoisted his bottle and quaffed deeply. Then, bug-eyed and almost breathless, he gasped . . . "Thunderation!" But the warm, comforting feeling that almost instantly coursed downward obviously inspired further investigation of this unexpected and delightful phenomena, and Thunderation Bill Ziem, the teetotaler, raised his bottle again, and again, and again. He noted, too, that cook Lecuyer and seamen Doar, Walther and Hendrickson had also discovered the rejuvenating wonders in the bottles urged upon them and were deeply immersed in their own experiments with the powerful and curative liquid.

Meanwhile, Captain Moore let the seas carry the lifeboat a hundred feet from the wreck before pulling away. Now faced with opposing seas in a course back to the tug, stroke oarsman Hough, shouting and counting faster than ever, slowly brought the lifeboat abeam of the tug where the hawser was once more secured. But entering the narrow harbor entrance with the lifeboat trailing astern from a different direction was out of the question. Just off the piers the line was again cast off and with the tug offering a lee of sorts the oarsmen brought their lifeboat in themselves. Most of those who had been watching from the bluffs had now gathered at the dock, and loud were the cheers for Captain Moore and his gallant crew as they stroked steadily in the calm waters of the harbor.

Mate George Hazelwood, meanwhile, after being hurried to the hotel for a hot bath and warm clothing, was provided with another bottle of the same life-giving fluid. He had experienced a remarkable recovery and was at the dock when many willing hands grasped for the lifeboat's lines. Local residents had energetically rounded up more clothing. While the sodden crew of the schooner were donning them in the privacy of the lifeboat station, there were numerous toasts to their saviors, the reunion with mate Hazelwood, the tug and Port Stanley people in general.

Ashore and with the full impact of the day's happenings slowly being impressed upon him, Captain Ziem grew philosophical and a bit garrulous, due, possibly, to the bottle he still clutched. "This is my first shipwreck in twelve years as a master. All my boys lost their money and all their good clothes. They're fine men, good steady workers who didn't throw their money away on drink. But you know, now that we have experienced disaster and the dreadful consequences of cold, I don't suppose it would do any harm to have a few bottles of this stuff aboard and handy-like, just in case of shipwreck, would it?"

Almost automatically or as in a prepared script, the participants in the recent drama repaired to the taproom of the Randall House, the local hostelry, there to be joined by villagers eager to offer their observation and experiences of that day and other days. Rooms for the shipwrecked crew had been obtained at the hotel, but for some reason all were reluctant to abandon the pleasant, once-in-a-lifetime camaraderie engendered by such a harrowing but special occasion.

When the witching hour of midnight drew near and the tenth recounting of specific deeds lost something of their original impact, there began a quiet shuffle for the door and oft-repeated "good nights."

But suddenly, from the cluster of hearties still three-deep around the bar, there came a loud and fervent voice which may or may not have come from Thunderation Bill Ziem.

"Jusht a moment, boys, before we go I wansht to osser a toasht . . . a toasht to the brave lifesh . . . er, lifeshavers."

---

1 In 1903 President Theodore Roosevelt recognized the heroism of the life-savers by authorizing "Presidential Gold Medals" for Captain J. Reginald Moore and crewmen William Hough, Henry Cherry, Alonzo Taylor, Thomas Hough, Fred Pollock and Frank Eveland. Captain Alex Brown of the tug *Gordon Brown* was the recipient of a gold watch and chain. The awards were presented by Dr. Wilson, a prominent physician and civic leader, at festivities attended by several thousand people. The last living member of the life-saving crew, Frank Eveland, still cherishing the beautiful medal, died in 1966 at the age of ninety-three.

# 11

## "Come Now, Mr. Manchester . . .
## Keep Going!"

THE PROPELLER *Jersey City* was about as functional as a vessel could be when she was launched in August of 1855. Built in Cleveland for the New York & Erie Railroad Company, she could accommodate a paying complement of passengers in comfort without minimizing her capacity to carry a variety of cargoes which, in her day, might range from crated cook stoves to bagged sugar and perhaps even a herd of cows. As a matter of fact she was advertised as being able to house two hundred head of cattle in addition to six thousand barrels of bulk cargo and other miscellaneous freight. Her two upright engines and ten-foot propellers were said to be equal to whatever might come her way in the way of cargo or weather. With great things and a long, prosperous life predicted for her, she began earning her keep in October, the intervening period required for interior finishing and fitting out. Captain J. G. Huff was her proud master.

Fate, however, has a deplorable habit of paying scant attention to favorable omens, confident predictions or ardent benedictions. The *Jersey City,* in what must be considered her "shake down" period, completed the season in good order, giving every indication of fulfilling all the expectations of her owners, builder and well-wishers.

The season of 1856 had scarcely begun when the vessel began to display a singular affinity for trouble. In May, when only a month out of her winter quarters, the *Jersey City* collided with the steamer *Minnesota* off Fairport, so seriously damaging the *Minnesota* that her crew had to quickly jettison over four hundred barrels of flour and whisky to keep her afloat.

Most of the 1857 season passed profitably and uneventfully, but in October and November the *Jersey City* again gave evidence of a perverse predilection for jousting with laws of survival. In October, while steaming among the islands in western Lake Erie, she struck a rock, opening up some seams. She was able to continue to Cleveland where the cargo was discharged, and the vessel was hauled out for repairs. But boats do not make money in repair yards and the time involved, about a week, was costly. Soon after resuming her labors she hit another rock, this one near the entrance to Dunkirk harbor. Again the leak was plugged but the *Jersey City* went into Buffalo for repairs that cost almost double the bill from the previous misadventure. A short time later it was another case of being in the wrong place at the wrong time. Buffalo was hit by a waterfront disaster caused by prolonged westerly winds raising the water level. At the same time hurricane-force winds mauled the vessels in the harbor, tearing them away from docks and causing numerous collisions. The *Jersey City* was rudely cuffed about, suffering considerable damage.

For two years a special dispensation from the fates spared the propeller from further embarrassing encounters with rocks, docks or other vessels. Possibly this was because the New York & Erie Railroad, like baseball-club owners when things are going badly, changed managers. Captain J. G. Huff was succeeded by Captain W. T. Monroe,[1] a well-known and popular master.

The 1860 season, like some of those earlier in the *Jersey City*'s still-short career, was successful up to a point. The point this time was the night of Friday, November 23, and Saturday, November 24. Poor Captain Monroe, the epitome of caution, could not have been expected to anticipate the sinister turn of events that transpired.

Late on the afternoon of the twenty-third, the Jersey City completed loading a diverse cargo at Cleveland, dominated by six thousand barrels of flour, pork, six hundred barrels of lard and a smaller burden of butter. A few passengers, ignoring the lateness of the season, also expressed a desire to go to Buffalo and booked passage. The weather was blustery but entirely in keeping with the season. Captain Monroe, busy with the manifold duties incumbent with command, could forsee no difficulties beyond those which faced every shipmaster in the waning days of a Great Lakes shipping season—a cold, forbidding sky, a sloppy bit of sea running and the necessity of seeing that the cargo was well secured with dunnage to prevent shifting. The times being what they were, he was in the position of every shipmaster afloat, entirely without the present-day conveniences and necessities of complete and accurate weather forecasts and other aids of navigation now taken for granted.

The weather, as the *Jersey City* departed Cleveland, was

not good, a strong southwest wind that built up seas, once the vessel was beyond the sheltered inshore waters, best described by sailors as "lumpy." When the *Jersey City* was well offshore and steaming eastward on the Buffalo course, they mounted in a diabolical and endless succession of rearing, foam-flecked following crests that came down upon the propeller like a relentless enemy, overpowering in numbers and dedicated to destruction. Unbeknownst to Captain Monroe, the following night and the succeeding day were to go down in history as one of the most destructive storms in Great Lakes history. Its force, unfortunately, concentrated on Lake Erie. He could not know, for example, that the propeller *Dacotah* would vanish during the night with all hands, and that a similar fate had already befallen the schooner *Hurricaine* in Lake Michigan. Captain Monroe's responsibility was to bring the *Jersey City* safely into Buffalo, and to that end he devoted his entire effort.

All night, as the steamer labored eastward, the storm grew in intensity, the increasing fury accompanied by a spectacular drop in temperature. As long as she stayed before the wind and seas the *Jersey City* suffered no more than heavy water over her decks, although the crests built up by the boisterous following seas caused her to pitch fearfully. At dawn the temperature was still falling and the cold air, meeting the warmer lake waters, generated furious snow squalls. A thin white rime of ice gave the *Jersey City* a frosted-cake appearance and the coating thickened moment by moment.

By mid-afternoon on November 24 Captain Monroe would have been the first to admit that he wasn't quite sure where he was. Like most vessels of her time, the *Jersey City* had a pilot house that boasted only a compass and clock as navigational aids. The rest was up to the skipper and his innate knowledge of the waters he was sailing. Captain Monroe knew that Long Point lay somewhere ahead, that deadly finger of sand that projected down from the north shore of Lake Erie to restrict the shipping channel and, far too often, to draw unwary sailors into the fatal embrace of its bars and sands. He had known many of its victims personally and did not want to further his knowledge of its hazards by personal experience.

At three o'clock that afternoon the *Jersey City* was but a white phantom on a dark panorama of tormented seas, their expanse mercifully hidden by blinding and intermittent snow squalls, driven on like frightened ghosts by a sixty-mile-per-hour gale. Captain Monroe had plotted a course that would take him clear of Long Point, but he knew that the following and slightly quartering seas would inevitably push his laboring boat northward. He had made allowances for that factor, but how far the *Jersey City* was being driven off her course was strictly a matter of educated guesswork.

Quite possibly it would have made no difference had the snow, driven on in biting, smothering blankets, hidden the navigational error from the eyes of the worried skipper. But suddenly there was a respite, and there it was before him, a tumultuous lather of white water as the towering breakers exploded on the bars and beaches of Long Point! The lighthouse at the very tip of the point was momentarily visible. It was by far the most terrifying sight Captain Monroe had ever encountered, but even in that moment of horror he mentally estimated how far off course the wind and seas had driven him and figured it to be about two miles. He had hoped earlier to round the point and anchor off the lee shore, but now here he was on the wrong side and most assuredly about to go aground!

Grabbing the wheel himself and rapidly swinging the *Jersey City* to starboard, he told the wheelsman to go below and tell the engineers and fireman how desperate their plight was. Down in the fire hold engineers Manchester and Cumming were already aware that a drastic alteration of course had been made for the vessel. Instead of pitching as she had when under assault by following seas, she was now rolling villainously in their troughs, the engines complaining to their very bed plates. But when the wheelsman had made known the desperate plight of both ship and crew, all hands turned to raising the steam pressure for a maximum effort. The gauges were already registering what would have been a highly satisfactory head of steam under normal conditions, but this was no time to hold to manufacturer's recommended figures. Some of the crew manhandled barrels of lard from the cargo down the engine room gratings and companionway. The lard, shoveled into the boilers, burned furiously, with the gauges reflecting a significant rise in pressure. The engines, despite the highly complimentary things said about them at the *Jersey City*'s launching, could do only so much, and on this terrible day of November 24, 1860, it was not enough!

Inevitably, and not much later than Captain Monroe's sighting of the dreaded beach, the *Jersey City* went hard on an offshore sand bar. Once able to roll with the punches, so to speak, she was now firm and immobile but no match for the high, marching seas that strode over her. Immediately upon impact Captain Monroe had ordered all hands topsides to the hurricane deck. If past experience was any criteria, from all he had heard, the hurricane deck would soon be

wrenched from the ship thus serving as a raft, its life expectancy admittedly of short duration, but possibly a means of saving lives. He was right. The fourth great sea plucked the deck away from the hull and drove it shoreward with passengers and crew desperately grasping whatever they could find for support. Undeterred by the disintegrating hull of the

*Jersey City,* the dark and frigid seas rolled right over the hurricane deck. Those clinging to it were numb, strength drained by the intense cold. It had been hoped that the plight of the vessel might have been witnessed by the light-keepers, but the interval of visibility that had enabled Captain Monroe to see the dreadful beach had been brief. The lightkeepers were further handicapped by a continuous cloud of sand blowing from the beach. So, as far as official knowledge of the wreck, the *Jersey City* went ashore in privacy.

Fifty yards from the beach the pitching hurricane deck went aground on another bar and the seas, coming in like mountains, quickly began to reduce the once-sturdy structure into mere driftwood. A young boy, one of the passengers, was washed overboard and Captain Monroe plunged in after him, clasping the lad in his arms and wading ashore through the surf. As he stood the boy upright the youngster's suspenders broke, his trousers dropping around his ankles, where they froze almost instantly. Captain Monroe tried to pull them up, but it was too late, the boy had already died.

Back through the hammering surf the captain fought his way to what was left of the hurricane deck to help his men and passengers ashore. Engineers Manchester and Cumming had already helped most of the *Jersey City*'s people through the surf. Finally only one, Albert H. Derby, the ship's clerk, remained on the sea-ravaged deck, his head bent down as though in utter despair. Unable even to talk, he was helpless as Manchester and second engineer Cumming helped hoist him on Captain Monroe's back. They wrapped his arms around the captain's neck and stood by to steady their skipper and his burden through the surf, which still broke over their heads. The snow had returned with a vengeance and the frigid wind blew furiously.

Once ashore Captain Monroe sought to lower the clerk, but found that Derby was dead and that his arms had frozen around his own neck and shoulders. The two engineers were too exhausted to help free him of his grisly cargo, so the captain had to fling himself to the sand, head first, thus spilling the dead clerk from his shoulders. But now he was in trouble himself. His trousers had frozen solid up to his hips, preventing him from rising. Nearby was the body of one of the passengers, frozen in a sitting position. Captain Monroe managed to roll himself to the body, using it as leverage to lift himself up.

The few survivors now began a short but tortuous march toward the lighthouse where they knew that shelter, food and warmth would be waiting.

First engineer Manchester was about done-in, pausing frequently to just stand there, shoulders sagging in utter exhaustion. But on each stop his assistant, Mr. Cumming, kept urging him on, sometimes walking beside him as support. Mr. Cumming was insistent in his pleas: "Come now, Mr. Manchester . . . keep going . . . keep going." Only a couple of hundred yards from their goal a small creek interrupted the trek. Under normal conditions it would not have mattered, but to men perilously close to death from exposure, it was almost an insurmountable canyon. First engineer Manchester attempted to cross it first but abandoned the effort to sit down in despair. Second engineer Cumming knelt beside him to help him up, murmuring, "Come now, Mr. Manchester, you've got to try again."

Neither one got up, freezing to death on the spot, faces

almost touching, as if each were whispering words of encouragement to the other. Like the two engineers, the other fifteen men lost had made the mistake of sitting down on the beach as soon as they crawled out of the surf, there to sit in death, lifeless puppets in a ghastly tableau, among the barrels and casks of flour, pork and lard.

Of the twenty-two aboard the *Jersey City* when she went aground only five survived—Captain Monroe, two firemen, a wheelsman and a single passenger. Eleven of the seventeen lost are still buried there in the shifting sands, somewhere near the lighthouse on Long Point.

---

1 Captain Monroe continued his Great Lakes career, commanding many other vessels. It is ironic, too, that several years after the *Jersey City* was lost, he was instrumental in saving the freezing crew of the *Omar Pasha*, stranded off Cleveland. Succeeding generations of Monroes continued to make their living on Lake Erie as commercial fishermen and, more recently, as operators of Monroe's Marina, at Barcelona, New York.

# 12

*Oddities and Odysseys*

Sᴀɪʟᴏʀs, probably because theirs is a lonely trade, are a superstitious and pessimistic lot, forever pinpointing significant coincidences, dates or a sequence of happenings and building them into myths, legends and fables, most of which have acquired some degree of authenticity merely by their frequent retelling. It was easy to pin the "unlucky" label on the 256-foot steamer *F. A. Meyer* simply because she made news with some regularity, usually as a result of some accident or as a pawn in court proceedings over ownership or proper division of her earnings. Built in Detroit in 1888 as the *J. Emory Owen* for the Corrigan fleet, she suffered a serious fire in an upper-lakes harbor and was subsequently sold and renamed. Although she carried substantial tonnages of many cargoes, the 1739 gross-ton *Meyer* was often employed in hauling stone from Kelleys Island, on Lake Erie, or lumber from any of a number of Michigan ports.

Her last trip through the legal machinations of admiralty court, in Cleveland, was on August 27, 1909, when she was attached as a result of action by Louis Pfohl of Buffalo. The

*Meyer* was jointly owned by Pfohl and Caroline Hartman, also of Buffalo. Mrs. Hartman's husband, Adam, also owned, wholly or in part, several other vessels, and presumably gave his wife the benefit of his judgment, experience and nautical expertise, none of which, apparently, boded well for the financial enrichment of Mr. Pfohl.

The task of attaching the *Meyer* by the usual routine of presenting the required legal documents fell to Deputy United States Marshal F. M. Fanning, a determined, ingenious man and an old hand at the game. The *Meyer,* the marshal found, had left Buffalo for Kelleys Island, towing one of the two barges she was usually encumbered with. The other barge, loaded with stone, had been dropped off at Cleveland on the previous trip. Marshal Fanning, through inquiries in the right circles in Buffalo, learned that the captain of the *Meyer,* Charles Kellar, had been instructed by Adam Hartman not to enter the harbor at Cleveland, but to anchor three miles out in the lake. Hartman would then charter a tug to tow the other barge out to the steamer, thus avoiding a confrontation with anyone who sought to attach or arrest her.

Early on the morning of the twenty-eighth the marshal appeared at the dock of the Great Lakes Towing Company to forestall the knave. He was too late. The chartered tug, with her unsuspecting skipper going about his work-a-day duties, was already abreast of the harbor piers, pulling the barge on a short line. With the alacrity for which the minions of the law are famous, the marshal immediately commandeered the tug *Lutz* and set off in pursuit. Unhindered by a barge, the *Lutz* soon overtook and passed the other tug, steaming full ahead to the anchored steamer. Although he fully expected trouble and was prepared to meet a hostile skipper and crew, the marshal found it unnecessary to draw his revolver when he boarded the vessel. Captain Kellar was presented with the seizure order and offered no resistance. Soon the *Meyer* and her barge, under tow by the *Lutz,* were headed into Cleveland harbor, followed by the other barge and her tug, the captain of which by now was utterly bewildered. By noon the steamer and her two consorts were at anchor inside the breakwall, legally forbidden to weigh anchor or move by order of the court.

The chagrined Adam Hartman beat a frantic path to the telegraph office, there to deal with Mr. Pfohl. The telegraph key clicked briskly all afternoon as the two litigants dickered by wire. Finally Pfohl agreed to surrender his interest in the embargoed vessel for a specified amount and so notified the admiralty court. The matter was settled.

Presumably the life of the *Meyer* was an easier one after the Cleveland fiasco, but it was not a long one. In December of 1910 she opened some seams while bucking ice in Lake Erie and went down. And while there was no loss of life, it didn't take apprehensive sailors and vesselmen long to compile the facts that would forever brand the *Meyer* as a "hoodoo" vessel. The number "13" was her downfall, they said, and recited many seemingly conspicuous incidents to document their claims. The *Meyer,* during the season of 1910, had actually had the audacity to sail from port on Friday, August 13! She carried a crew of thirteen men, was insured for $13,000, and, on her last voyage, carried 1,300,000 board feet of lumber!

Actually, the *Meyer* had completed her season and was about to be laid up on December 1, when Adam Hartman received an attractive offer to move a cargo of lumber from Rouge Bay, on Lake Michigan, to a Lake Erie port. Although her seasonal insurance had lapsed and could not be renewed, the *Meyer* steamed to Lake Michigan with the same thirteen-man crew that had been aboard all year. She was seemingly "home free" when the destructive ice floes were encountered back on Lake Erie. And it follows, of course, that she foundered on the thirteenth!

## II

It was the number "7" that figured significantly in the life and times of the late Captain Hugh Donald McLeod, a man who held captain's papers for seventy-three of his ninety-four years. Perhaps there was a mystical preordination factor involved. He was the seventh son of a seventh son.

Hugh Donald McLeod was among the very last of an almost vanished breed of lake sailors who shipped before the mast in wooden schooners and lived to command the steel bulk-carrying monsters of today. Strangely, through the years —sixty-nine of them—he was on the fleet payroll of but one company which, after various amalgamations, is now known as the United States Steel Corporation.

The fateful number seven and the singular fashion with which it is interwoven in the fabric of the McLeod family challenges the imagination and the laws of probability.

The sinister influence of the number begins on December 7, 1909, when the big carferry *Marquette & Bessemer No. 2* steamed out of Conneaut, Ohio, bound for Port Stanley, Ontario. Aboard, as master, was Captain Robert McLeod, Captain Hugh's brother. Another brother, John, although a skipper in his own right, was acting as first mate. The carferry departed in the face of a stiff Lake Erie gale and disappeared from the face of the earth, never again to be seen by mortal man!

On the following seventh of April, the Conneaut newspaper reported that the body of John McLeod had been found in the Niagara River, encased in ice. Six months later, again on the seventh, Captain Hugh McLeod was called to Long Point. Captain Robert McLeod's body had been found there on the sandy beach. In both instances it had fallen the lot of Captain Hugh to go to the scene to make positive identification.

The captain's next brush with the ill-fated number seven was on April 7, 1914, when he was master of the whaleback steamer *John Ericsson*. The *Ericsson* was towing the whaleback barge *Alexander Holly* down Lake Huron, but, due to storm and fog, the only evidence that the barge was properly following her steamer was the tight towing wire strung out aft. After lunch that day Captain McLeod walked to the fantail to see if he could sight the *Alexander Holly*. During a momentary break in the fog he noticed that the barge's flag was flying at half-mast. Captain McLeod immediately ordered the steamer's speed reduced and winched in the towing cable until the barge was close enough to permit conversation with the watchman who suddenly appeared on the forepeak. Then, and only then, did he learn that the captain of the barge had been washed overboard the day before!

It was also significant, and duly noted by Captain Hugh McLeod, that Murdena McLeod, wife of the late Captain Robert, was buried in Detroit on October 7, 1941, and that on October 7, 1961, her youngest daughter, Charlotte, was buried. Captain Robert's daughter, Belle, died seven years after her own daughter, Josephine, passed away, and seven weeks before her husband died.

On the happier side Captain Hugh recalled that October 7 was the birthday of one of Captain Robert's granddaughters and also the birthday of one of his own daughters.

From cabin boy to master, Captain Hugh McLeod served on a known twenty-six vessels during his long career, his final command being the big *D. G. Kerr*. It is typical of the fates that had plagued him with a number fraught mostly with disaster that he would retire on a day that would be historic not only for him, but for the nation. For even as he bid adieu to the *Kerr* the Japanese were bombing Pearl Harbor. It was December 7, 1941!

### III

During the years he spent as keeper of the Mamajuda and Grassy Island lighthouses on the lower Detroit River, Gus Gramer became quite a favorite with newspaper reporters. He was in the headlines many times, usually as a result of daring rescues of blundering yachtsmen or saving inebriated fishermen from the perils of the deep. Because he was rough, gruff, irreverent and not above a bit of ribald embellishment, he was always good "copy."

But when he was transferred to the Toledo harbor light, as keeper-in-charge, he almost immediately fell afoul his assistant, a quite proper and by-the-book fellow. After weeks of quarreling, the assistant, unable to tolerate Gus's abrasive manner and contempt for regulation procedures, wrote an anguished letter to Washington, preferring charges. And when

Roscoe House, chief clerk in the Buffalo office of the light-house service, came to investigate the matter, Gus, according to the investigator, became abusive and insolent, going so far as to tell Mr. House to "go to hell." Mr. House, properly outraged, therefore notified Washington of the situation, thus triggering a hearing in Toledo, an official affair Gus refused to dignify with his presence. Upon being found guilty as charged and so notified of his suspension, he steadfastly refused to vacate the lighthouse premises and turn over all government property to his successor, as ordered. Whereupon the aggrieved Mr. House returned to Toledo in the same tug he had chartered to apprise Gus of his suspension, there enlisting the aid of United States Marshal Wagner. Marshal Wagner, a direct actionist, enlisted the aid of two Toledo detectives and with the fuming Mr. House reboarded the tug, the expedition dedicated to the task of evicting the obstinate rascal defying duly constituted authority. All were heavily armed in event Gus decided to make a fight of it. But poor old Gus, his time and luck running out, noted the array of armament and decided to abdicate.

He said not a word on the rough return journey, but as the tug's lines were being snaked out to the dock and only when the waiting newspapermen were within earshot, he gave off the final quip he calculated would give one more, and perhaps his last, headline.

"Hell," he roared, "you guys can't fire me . . . I quit!"

## IV

During the grim, demoralizing days of the Great Depression, with the demand for iron ore, limestone and coal vastly diminished, hundreds of sailors were "on the beach," their own unique terminology for being unemployed. Aboard the few vessels that did sail, the old rule of seniority prevailed as fleet operators tried to keep as many of their licensed men working as was possible, whatever their previous rank. Vessels steamed away from winter mooring ports with shipmasters working as watchmen and chief engineers serving as oilers and wipers.

Nor was the prestigious Cleveland-Cliffs Iron Company fleet an exception. Marine manager A. E. R. Schneider was hard put to find gainful employment for all his licensed men, as some of the company's boats were fitted out much later than usual. Still other boats were laid up long before the traditional late November or early December dates.

In 1931 a case in point was that of Captain A. J. Rathbun who, for the three previous seasons, had been master of the steamer *Yosemite*. He started out as a wheelsman on the *Cadillac* and *Pontiac* as they were being fitted out; went next to the *J. H. Sheadle* as watchman before being transferred to the *Cadillac* as second mate. Soon he was sent back to the *J. H. Sheadle,* but still as second mate. His next berth was first mate on the *Pam Schneider* before once more regaining a master's assignment, first on the *Colonel* and then on the *Yosemite*. After another move to first mate on the *Pontiac* he again went as master of the *Marquette* and later the *J. H. Sheadle*. At lay-up time he was first mate again, first on the *Peter White* and later the *Ishpeming*. In all, during the 1931 season he had various positions on nine boats, fitting out seven and laying up two.

V

Mutiny is a nasty word, particularly in naval circles, inspiring all sorts of ugly implications and unpleasant visions of condemned sailors in chains or dangling from the yardarms of ships of war. Captains of such vessels were traditionally harsh taskmasters, firm in their convictions that discipline could be maintained only by severe beatings, often for minor offenses and preferably with the entire crew as witness. Even the hint of acts or words that could be interpreted as defiant or mutinous in nature were seemingly justification for savage whippings or keelhauling. Likewise, skippers of merchant vessels of another era were firm believers in the stern, no-nonsense approach to managing their crews, although the bucko mates usually handled the physical punishment with their fists, singling out the alleged miscreants for insolence or misdeeds, real or imagined. The history of seafaring is replete with documented records of cruel and inhuman punishment dealt out to sailors when very often the real culprits were the officers who drove their men relentlessly while providing them with what could only be considered starvation, scurvy-inducing diets by today's standards.

Instances of mutiny on the Great Lakes are few, but not nearly as rare as one would imagine. But what would be considered mutinous acts on naval or merchant vessels on the high seas were, on freshwater, often more accurately termed revolts or protests. Consequently they lost the sinister glamour so often associated with more-publicized occasions when sailors defied their captains or officers. Many individuals merely deserted ship by jumping overboard when in confined waters such as the Detroit or St. Clair rivers; others waited until they reached a convenient port of call. And so very frequently, food, the lack of, or quality of, was the primary cause for such protest, desertion or revolt.

The crew of the steamer *Forest City* left the ship en masse upon its arrival at Port Stanley, Ontario, after a rough trip from Cleveland in July of 1910. Dock workers who questioned the sailors found that the trouble was partly because of low wages but mostly a unanimous unhappiness with the food being served them. Twelve of the crew of thirteen immediately left the boat with all their gear, boarding a train for Sarnia. Only the captain, first mate and chief engineer were left aboard the *Forest City* to do with her what they would.

### VI

Excitement reigned supreme one morning at Duncan's dock along the Port Huron waterfront when the cook of the steamer *Rhoda Emily* missed two hams and accused Roy Bissel, a deckhand, of taking them. The cook, cleaver in hand, waxed eloquent on the subject of Bissel's forebears and Bissel was equally vociferous in his denial of the deed and his suspicions as to the cook's ancestors. The crew, however, sided to a man with the deckhand and walked off the ship in a body. For nearly an hour they argued and exchanged words with the *Rhoda Emily*'s captain and officers, returning to their duties eventually, but only after the cook had been discharged and a replacement signed on.

### VII

Food, the quality, quantity and frequency thereof, was apparently the source of trouble aboard the big ore carrier

*Douglass Houghton,* downbound in mid-Lake Michigan one warm day in August of 1910. In any event the crew mutinied, firemen, oilers, even wheelsmen deserting their posts of duty while the 456-foot steamer of the Pittsburgh Steamship Company fleet, her big engine idle, drifted at the mercy of wind and wave. Locked in their staterooms during the progress of the uprising, badly frightened and fearful lest the captain and his officers be overpowered by the unruly crewmen, were six young women from the Chicago area, making a pleasure trip on the freighter. Reason prevailed after the captain, pistol in hand, confronted the exceedingly disgruntled sailors and succeeded in mollifying them. The matter was rather successfully hushed up, but the scuttlebutt in the waterfront hangouts was that the galley crew was dreadfully incompetent and entirely too penurious with hearty, stick-to-the-ribs steamboat food!

## VIII

Food was high on the priority list of one anonymous seaman who, in 1923, took pen in hand to rectify what was obviously a bit of chicanery in the galley department of the steamer *Fontana* of the Cleveland-Cliffs fleet. Strangely, too, for Cleveland-Cliffs has always been known for the fine table they set and the culinary skills of their stewards.

Hotel Tomkins
Toledo, Ohio

Cleveland Cliffs Iron Co.
   Sirs:
      I have sailed on most all of your boats but the *Fontana* is the worse'd I have ever been on. There is no meat served

at all, kindly look into this as I know it is not the Company's fault so somebody is sure getting a rake off.

(signed)   A sailor

## IX

Food was certainly not a factor in the donnybrook that nearly got the captain of the sidewheel steamer *John A. Dix* hanged on his own masthead; it was the lack of human compassion on his part.

The *Dix,* originally built as a cutter for the U.S. Revenue Service, was later sold to a commercial operator. Her powerful Murphy beam engine was so efficient that she normally towed a barge behind her, sometimes two of them. Such was the case in the fall of 1872 when the *Dix* was downbound on Lake Superior. Behind her trailed the loaded barges *Saturn* and *Jupiter,* the latter with the popular Captain Peter Howard in command. All went well until the steamer and her consorts passed Keweenaw Point when a fair-to-middlin' northwest gale swept down upon them. They were beyond the point of no return to the shelter offered in the lee of Keweenaw, and, under the circumstances, there was little to do but plug on, hoping to weather the long, weary miles to Whitefish Point where, once around the point, similar shelter and good holding ground were to be found. But the seas continued to grow in stature and the eighteen-year-old steamer began to roll heavily and pound. Night brought no relief but only an intensified awareness on the part of the skipper that should either or both of the barges founder in the darkness, a calamity he considered quite likely, they might drag the *Dix* under with them. At midnight, although many of his crew considered the action precipitous, he ordered the towing hawser severed and the barges cast adrift to shift for themselves. Free of its burden the *Dix* responded more readily to the lift of the seas and in due time slipped behind Whitefish Point to find respite from the gale. The crew was aware that the barges were equipped with adequate ground tackle and were quite capable of surviving considerable weather. So they naturally assumed that once the emergency had passed, the captain would retrace the steamer's track and make some attempt to locate and recover the barges and their crews. The captain had other thoughts, however, and when the seas subsided he steamed the *Dix* into Sault Ste. Marie, there to tie up to a convenient berth.

Scarcely had the *Dix* been secured when a committee of crewmen respectfully asked the captain to return to Lake Superior and conduct a search for the *Saturn* and *Jupiter* and their people. He steadfastly and adamantly refused, although he could offer no reason the men considered valid or sincere. The incensed and bitter crew, once they got ashore, quickly transmitted their feelings of rage and frustration to other sailors and to sympathetic townspeople. In a relatively short time tempers, perhaps inflamed by spirits, were running so high that a posse of aroused sailors and citizens gathered to begin a march to the steamer's moorings. It was the firm determination of those so employed to hang the skipper to his own masthead, an action they viewed as just and deserving in light of his callous disregard for the lives of the men on the barges. Through some happenstance, however, the captain of the *Dix* heard of the ominous trend of events and hastily hiring a horse and buggy owned by a local Indian, fled southward in the still watches of the night.

As it developed, a search for the people of the *Saturn* and

*Jupiter* would have been fruitless. Long before the gale had blown itself out, both barges had gone ashore, one off the Two Hearted River, the other near Clark's Creek, at Whitefish Point, thirty and fifty miles, respectively, from where they had been cast adrift. All hands, including Captain Peter Howard of the *Jupiter,* were lost!


## X

Captain John Dorrington of Detroit was one of the old school of masters who, in the course of time, came to own their own vessels, in his case the 175-foot schooner *Maria Martin.* The heyday of sailing craft was long over when Captain Dorrington assumed command and ownership of the *Maria Martin,* but she still carried lumber, fence posts, cordwood, stone, potatoes and a variety of other cargoes with efficiency. She always earned her own keep, as sailors and shipowners say, despite her advanced age. Built in Cleveland in 1866, she was old when he bought her and by the usual mortality tables applied to sailing craft should long since have gone to the boneyard. But Captain Dorrington was well aware of her infirmities and never demanded more of her than she could deliver. He kept his weather eye peeled, hauling for shelter when the barometer indicated boisterous conditions. Her earnings, in the face of competition from steamboats, were marginal, compelling her skipper frequently to sail short-handed and to abstain from using tugs whenever possible, even when prudence sometimes dictated otherwise. Tugboats, he once confided to a fellow skipper, were part of a dreadful conspiracy of steamship owners to drive the schooner operators into bankruptcy.

One violent November night in 1906 the winds pulled the *Maria Martin* from her home-port moorings and swept her down the Detroit River. Captain Dorrington, the only man aboard, got ashore in a small boat and called the local fire tug which made a valiant effort to save her. The captain had hoped she would pass safely through the draw of the Belle Isle bridge, thus giving him more time to corral his schooner, but the bridge tender, fearing catastrophic damage to the structure should the craft be swept broadside into the open draw, ignored the captain's frantic pleas. In any event the *Maria Martin* "took the ground" on a blue clay shoal. The brisk current promptly swung her around, putting her hard-on for practically her full length. It was a calamity but one that could not be avoided. Had the captain immediately called for assistance from the dreaded steam tugs the schooner could have been quickly liberated. But day after day and week after week the *Maria Martin* sat there in the mud, immobilized and forlorn as commerce passed her by and Captain Dorrington waited for a miracle to take her off. While waiting for the miracle, he made several attempts to kedge his vessel from the shoal, but his ground tackle was not substantial enough. Heavier equipment and men to operate it came at a pretty price, much more, in fact, than the tugs would have charged had they put lines aboard soon after the stranding. Meanwhile, the persistent current had piled up more mud and silt around the hull until the *Maria Martin* was no longer a simple towing job. By now her salvage had become a major operation with considerable dredging required to free her. Winter came, passed, and another season found the schooner still in her bed of mud, and the good captain still adamant. When it became apparent that she was going to be a fixture for some time, several enterprising Detroit clothing firms persuaded the captain to permit them to paint advertising signs on the hull, crying out the merits of their goods. The price was fair and with his schooner earning not a penny, he readily acquiesced.

To the official forces responsible for maintaining the waterways and their markings, the appearance of the signs was evidence that the captain had abandoned all hope of his vessel ever sailing again. They therefore demanded that he surrender the vessel for removal as a hazard to navigation. Threats and legal maneuvers went on for another two years, the captain always promising action but backing down when marine salvagers presented their estimates for freeing the *Maria Martin*.

At long last the government took the bull by the horns, so to speak, officially declaring the *Maria Martin* to be a navigational hazard and awarding a contract to remove her, at government expense, to David M. Hackett. Captain Dorrington, who had the sympathies of many, immediately enlisted the help of old friends to come aboard and help him defend his vessel against an expected hostile force. By his own calculations the captain figured that the government, if they wanted his vessel removed, should pay him a satisfactory sum. Rather than a navigational hazard, he pointed out to newsmen, he considered the schooner to be a navigational aid as it clearly marked a dangerous shoal the official people had deigned to mark only with a single spar buoy. Moreover, he pointed out in some heat, the stranded schooner had become a haven of mercy and rescue for the occupants of capsized small boats, and, on several occasions, had undoubtedly saved lives.

The invading force Captain Dorrington expected came in the form of the tug *Aldrich* and the wrecking vessel *Mills,* both under command of Captain Fred Trotter of Amherstburg, hired for the job by Hackett. The besieging vessels tied up to the schooner, but only Captain Trotter was permitted to climb aboard and then only long enough for the schooner's skipper to inform him that any attempt to remove his vessel would be resisted with force, gunfire, if necessary.

"Let the government take possession," he advised Captain Trotter. "That is, if they can."

Obviously chagrined at his reception, Captain Trotter withdrew his tug and wrecking vessel, retreating to the Canadian side of the river to await instructions. Captain Dorrington had won the first round!

Outraged at the turn of events, Mr. Hackett appealed to the proper authorities, complaining bitterly that they had not informed him of the unusual hazards involved in removing the hulk of the *Maria Martin,* or the risk to life and limb by actions of her determined skipper.

The atmosphere surrounding the affair, with the embattled captain obviously enjoying the attention, was supercharged for the next few days. A government launch was seen darting out to the stranded schooner several times, its occupants apparently having heated debates with Captain Dorrington.

Finally the wrecker *Mills* and the tug *Aldrich* steamed up the river once more, mooring to the *Maria Martin* without fisticuffs or gunfire. The launch appeared again, too, and Captain Dorrington was seen to board her, after which the little craft sped for shore. It was noted by waiting newsmen and interested spectators, as the launch approached the dock, that a grinning Captain Dorrington was holding up an impressive and obviously official bit of paper which looked suspiciously like a government check!

## XI

Of all the shipping companies that flourished on the Great Lakes in earlier years, none was held in greater esteem than the old Anchor Line. Operators of a fine fleet of passenger vessels and package freighters, the company set high standards for the seaworthiness of its boats, maintenance of equipment, qualifications of its officers, and, most important to sailors, set a good and hearty table. But as always in a smartly run organization, on the boat the captain's word was law, and his eccentricities, assuming they were within reason, prevailed.

One of the senior skippers, a venerable and highly experienced mariner, held that his enviable state of health in advancing years was due solely to his daily consumption of prunes, the efficacy of which he enthusiastically recommended to all mortals. He went so far as to insist that stewards on vessels he commanded make them available at every meal. So determined were his efforts to promote the fruit that years after both he and his company had become part of history, prunes on shipboard were referred to as "Anchor Line strawberries."

## XII

The mysteries of the Great Lakes are not always confined to vanished vessels and their crews, but sometimes involved individuals whose perplexing thoughts or actions, and the reasons for them, were known but to themselves.

At 10:15 on the night of April 28, 1937, Captain George R. Doner of the steamer *O. M. McFarland* left the pilot house, giving instructions to the second mate to call him when the *McFarland* was off her destination of Port Washington, Wisconsin, some three hours hence. Stating that he wanted to get a couple of hours of sleep, he went below, out of sight of the mate and wheelsman. The desire for rest was understandable, for the *McFarland,* on her first trip of the season, had encountered the usual heavy ice in the Straits of Mackinac, losing considerable time. And once in northern Lake Michigan a sharp watch had to be kept for roving ice fields. Under the existing conditions, Captain Doner, as befits a conscientious master, had spent many long sleepless hours in the pilot house. The *McFarland,* one of the Columbia Transportation Company's crane vessels, had loaded coal at Erie, Pennsylvania, 5800 tons of it.

The voyage to Port Washington might have been considered routine by many shipmasters, but it was something special for the captain. It was his first command under the Columbia house flag, although he had been on the lakes for years and had served as a skipper for several of them. He had sailed for ten years on the old Valley Camp Steamship Company's boats until the firm was taken over by Columbia. But his new employers, while valuing his long experience, had a surfeit of qualified shipmasters and had assigned him mate's duties until time and attrition in the ranks brought him once more a command.

After leaving the pilot house Captain Doner must have busied himself with paper work before retiring, for he was later heard moving around in his room. At 1:15 A.M., as the *McFarland* neared Port Washington, the mate, as instructed, descended to the captain's room to call him. There was no response to his knocking on the door so the second officer opened it and peered in, assuming that the captain was merely sleeping heavily. But Captain Doner was not in his bed or anywhere else in sight. On the possibility that the captain had walked aft to get coffee or partake of the night lunch, the mate hurried back to the galley, but except for a couple of off-duty firemen finishing a midnight snack, it was deserted. Quickly summoning the other mate and the chief engineer he organized a thorough search of the *McFarland,* crew members combing every nook and cranny of the thirty-four-year-old vessel. Without a doubt, Captain Doner had disappeared!

Beyond the fact that their captain had "seemed a little nervous," not a single member of the crew could advance a logical reason for his "going over the side," which is certainly what must have happened. Nor could the Coast Guard people who came aboard at Port Washington ascribe any reason or circumstances that would impel a shipmaster, particularly one recently appointed, to take such action. Could it have been an accident? Such things had happened before. When it was later learned that he had been suffering from a heart condition for four years, this solution achieved some status of credibility. Perhaps he had indeed decided to walk aft for coffee and had experienced a seizure, causing him to plunge over the low rail, actually cable strung through removable uprights. But the mate, aware that his commander was extremely tired, doubted very much that he had gone aft for coffee.

Whatever the reason, accident or no, Captain Doner was gone. Shortly after docking, the thoughtful mate had a watchman lower the *McFarland*'s flag to half-mast in respect for the missing skipper. It was something Captain Doner would have appreciated, coming as it did on his fifty-eighth birthday!

## XIII

Much has been said and written, perhaps too much, of the days of wooden ships and iron men. Usually the yarns compare the present with a period when most vessels were indeed of wood and their crews, by the very nature of their tasks and shipboard surroundings, led a Spartan existence. But there were men of iron in the pilot houses too, men of iron wills and consummate skills. In an era when the only pilot-house aids were a clock, compass and steering wheel, they performed feats of navigation that would be considered remarkable even today. And because they had learned their trade at an early age and added to their knowledge by experience acquired in long and often bitter processes, they achieved that mysterious quality of inspired decision making known as "instinct," a term nobody has been able to define successfully. Nor, for that matter, is there a substitute for this elusive qualification for a shipmaster, one that would enable him to serve his owners or the men whose lives were in his trust so well.

Such an instinctive skipper was Captain Dave Beggs of the 180-foot wooden steamer *Aztec*. Anticipating nothing out of the ordinary, Captain Beggs departed Chicago one day at the turn of the century with a cargo of grain destined for Montreal. But scarcely had the *Aztec* cleared port and set course for the long haul up the east coast of Lake Michigan when a dense fog set in, the worst he or any member of the crew could recall. For many weary hours the *Aztec* crawled along in a gray and silent world with no visibility beyond her bow. Even the stern of the vessel was lost in impenetrable murk that had fallen over Lake Michigan. Except for the rhythmic bleating of her whistle and the thrashing of her propeller, the boat made not a sound. All the way up the lake and through the dreaded Grays Reef passage, Captain Beggs piloted the *Aztec* by dead reckoning, using the only tools at his command—the clock to tell him how long he had been steaming on a specific course, the taffrail log to record the distance traveled and frequent reports from the mate who regularly manned the sounding lead.

At the Straits of Mackinac, the wreck-strewn bottleneck passage between Lake Michigan and Lake Huron, the *Aztec* was still in a fog as thick as cotton. With the pilot-house windows all open, the mournful hooting of a half-dozen other vessels could be heard, some obviously in the distance, others ominously nearby. It was Captain Beggs' responsibility to judge their course and proximity, relying on a mental reflex action that comes from a strange capability known only as instinct. The fog was as thick as ever, but somehow, nobody knew how or why, the vessel came through safely, hauled to starboard and began the long trek down Lake Huron. Still the fog persisted, if anything even worse. There were times when the bow watchman, standing and listening only a few feet forward of the pilot house, could be heard but not seen.

Then came more long and sleepless hours during which Captain Beggs stared at the clock with bloodshot eyes, recorded the readings from the taffrail log and compared his charts with the reports from the mate, still systematically dropping the sounding lead and calling up the depths and the characteristics of the bottom—mud, sand or gravel. According to his calculations the *Aztec* should at last be nearing the crucial area where the shipping lanes converge as Lake Huron ends and the swift and narrow St. Clair River begins. But something, an important something, was missing! The loud and welcome blasting of the fog whistle on the Lake Huron lightship, stationed a couple of miles lakeward of the river, could not be heard, yet it had to be there somewhere. Unknown to those aboard the *Aztec,* the signal whistle was out of order and had been silent for several hours. Frantic efforts were being made aboard the lightship to effect repairs on a broken valve. The fog had grown so dense the captain found it difficult to discern the handrails outside the pilot house door. He had by now checked his vessel down to dead slow. Another sounding with the lead convinced him that he was exactly where he thought he should be, not far from Port Huron and the entrance to the St. Clair River. Still no sobbing of the whistle from the lightship!

Suddenly, and it had to be instinct again, Captain Beggs knew he could take the *Aztec* no farther. He rang the engine room for "stop" and ordered the mate to drop the anchors. Down they went with a great clatter and clanking, the mate making sure they had "grabbed" and the way was off the ship before securing the chain with an iron pin jammed through a link. For the first time in days the *Aztec* lay motionless on the flat, fog-shrouded water her people could sense but not see.

Heaving a sigh of relief, Captain Beggs resigned himself

for what could be a long wait, but before taking to his bed for a well-deserved nap he instructed the mate to have a man scrub the soot and grime from the steering pole while it was still wet and dripping from the moisture of the fog. The seaman assigned to the task sought to raise the steering pole with the tackle provided but complained that it wouldn't work.

"Let it go for now," the mate grumbled.

The rather abrupt shift of the wind that quickly dispersed the fog brought a heart-stopping moment, not only for Captain Beggs, but for all who had placed implicit trust in his remarkable seamanship. For it revealed why the steering pole had been reluctant to respond to the hoisting tackle. The "shark's tail" at the outer end of the pole was firmly fouled in the rigging of the Huron lightship!

It was a startling sight, the ultimate triumph of that mysterious something called instinct.

## XIV

Joseph C. Gilchrist was a deckhand at sixteen, a lumber-yard proprietor at twenty-two, owner of his first schooner at thirty and a shipping magnate when still a comparatively young man. The key to his success, although sour-grapes rivals hinted that luck was an important factor, was really a shrewd sense of business combined with abounding energy and unshakable faith in the future of Great Lakes shipping.

Starting with the purchase of the 500-ton schooner *Stafford,* soon followed by the acquisition of the *Benton,* he accumulated vessels rapidly—schooners, barges and wooden steamers. Before long, during lean years, he was purchasing boats in lots—seven wooden steamers of the Wilson fleet, six more and a steel steamer from a Detroit estate and another group of five steel steamers from a liquidating Buffalo firm. He also had a persuasive way of convincing others to invest in his firm, and before long he headed an active partnership organization which included his cousin, Frank W. Gilchrist, of Alpena, Michigan.

Buying vessels is a relatively simple matter if one has the resources. Keeping them gainfully employed, even in good years, is an infinitely rarer accomplishment. But Joseph C. Gilchrist, with his bubbling enthusiasm and a host of influential friends in all phases of lake shipping, did just that, managing to find cargoes of coal, ore, stone or grain for a mostly aged fleet while more modern bottoms were tied up for lack of business. He consistently operated as an "independent," shunning seasonal commitments which would have tied up some of his vessels late in the year when coal traffic was booming and when grain-hauling rates and winter-storage cargoes were particularly lucrative. In 1903 the Gilchrist fleet moved 4,657,603 tons of bulk freight, much of it coal, and also carried one-seventh of all the grain brought to the port of Buffalo, then the country's largest milling center.

Beyond the remarkable record of activity for his vessels, 1903 was to be another example of Gilchrist luck, if it could be called that, this time with a reverse twist. Prior to 1903 the Gilchrist vessels had not been covered by formal insurance, the hull and cargo premiums, particularly for the older boats, being deemed prohibitive. Many large fleets, including the Gilchrist line were, instead, "self-insured," the operators setting aside a certain percentage of earnings to cover loss, damage or subsequent litigation. Perhaps it was that instinctive something or other that business geniuses possess, or possibly a hunch, but in any event Gilchrist yielded to the blandishments of a persistent marine-insurance salesman, and for the first time in its history his fleet was covered against any and all contingencies. And well it was, too, for what happened to Gilchrist vessels that year, mostly in Lake Superior, boggles the mind.

Late in July the twenty-nine-year-old steamer *V. Swain* sprang a leak at Two Harbors and sank at her dock, precipitating a raising and refurbishing operation that cost $12,000. On September 17 the venerable schooner barge *Moonlight* foundered off Michigan Island on the first day of a three-day blow. Two days later the wooden steamer *A. A. Parker* went down off Grand Marais with the loss of vessel and cargo said to be in the neighborhood of $75,000. On October 15 the *Marquette,* another veteran of the Gilchrist fleet, suddenly foundered off the Apostle Islands with a $60,000 loss. Eleven days later the *Manhattan* stranded at Grand Island, fire breaking out immediately and burning her to the water line. The wheat cargo had been insured for $65,000 and the vessel valued at $50,000. Two other wooden Gilchrist steamers, the 275-foot *John Craig* and the 191-foot *Waverly,* were lost elsewhere, but whatever the circumstances or however amicable the settlements, 1903 must have been a traumatic year for a certain insurance salesman.

## XV

Ship captains have called anathemas down upon the heads of steamboat inspectors for years, but a Buffalo skipper, after vociferously denouncing the official gentlemen, had good and sufficient cause for later reversing his position, concluding that their prompt and stern judgment undoubtedly saved his life.

On September 11, 1907, Captain Frank Bertrand was in command when the steamer *Alexander Nimick* departed Buffalo for Lake Superior ports. Shortly after clearing the harbor the *Nimick* encountered such violent weather that Captain Bertrand, deeming caution the better part of valor, chose to return to port. The decision was probably very wise, but while retracing his tracks the *Nimick* came into collision with the steamer *S. S. Curry*. The inspectors viewed the incident with a jaundiced eye and quickly found Captain Bertrand guilty of an outrageously bungled bit of seamanship, suspending him for thirty days.

The *Nimick* finally resumed her voyage but this time with Captain John Randall at the helm. A few days later the vessel sprang a leak and was lost on Lake Superior. Captain Randall and five men perished with her!


XVI

On the afternoon of May 16, 1937, grain trimmer Wesley Taylor was accidentally buried in the after hold of the steamer *W. J. Connors* while the vessel was loading oats at Duluth's Peavey elevator. His absence not noted by his fellow workers, Taylor lay submerged by the grain as the steamer finished loading, clearing for Buffalo early in the evening. Meanwhile, the frightened grain timmer managed to claw his way to the after bulkhead where he frantically began rapping on the metal to attract attention. The chief engineer, an astute fellow, quickly deduced what had happened and notified the *Connors'* master who ordered the wheelsman to turn the vessel back to port. At the elevator the spouts removed 4000 bushels of oats before Taylor could grasp a rope lowered to him. Little the worse for his experience, he ate his supper aboard the *Connors,* after which he was taken to his home, one of the few men to have survived such an ordeal.

## XVII

Rarely has a man's appetite proved fatal, but for Charles Smith, a deck hand on the steamer *Cuyler Adams,* such was the case on the evening of November 9, 1926. Smith, who had signed on only a week before, was properly indignant when a storm which developed shortly after the steamer left Duluth kept him and other crewmen virtually prisoners in their forward quarters for a full day and night as mountainous seas continually swept the deck of the *Cuyler Adams.* Finally, declaring to his shipmates that he might as well die of too much water as too little food, Smith started a perilous journey over the ice-coated decks at dinner time, heading for the crew's mess in the after cabins. A huge sea, curling in from the northwest, came romping in over the deck, and Smith, despite the lifeline rigged for just such dangerous excursions, disappeared in the crest of the sea and was seen no more!

## XVIII

In the mid-nineteenth century the "Queen's Bush" was a term applied to untold millions of acres of wilderness land in Canada, large blocks of which were given away or sold for a pittance to opportunists and reigning government favorites. More was handed out to others who had been of some service to the Crown, in lieu of gratuities, and to discharged soldiers and navy men. Field officers were given 5000 acres, captains 2000, and private soldiers 200. The clergy, magistrates, barristers, executive councilors, legislative councilors and even those who surveyed the lands also came in for large holdings.

The land allotted to soldiers, many of whom never saw their property, was bought up for a pittance by speculators or land jobbers, some of them high-ranking government officials, military officers and members of Parliament. They made, in every instance, fortuitous purchases that paid off handsomely in the years to come. The lands, escalated in value but still cheap, brought a flood tide of immigrants to Canada, a large proportion of them from the British Isles.

The total failure of the potato crop of 1847–1848 drove many Irishmen from their homeland to seek a better way of life in the "Queen's Bush."

In the same wave of migration came disgruntled Scots by the thousands. The group important to our story are those from the island of Lewis, off the northwest coast of Scotland. It was one of the largest "block" settlements to pull up stakes en masse. Ownership of property in the British Isles in the eighteenth and nineteenth centuries was almost an exclusive privilege of the wealthy or titled. Those not in this envious category faced, as their ancestors had, a life of virtual serfdom, their futures entirely in the hands of others. Migration to new homes in the colonies, Australia or the Queen's Bush, in Canada, was the only way out.

The people of the island of Lewis, who had farmed their croftings and fished, were evicted by their landlord, Sir James

Matheson, who apparently sought to convert his acreage to gamekeeping and private deer preserves. It was a heartless act, and Sir James, apparently suffering twinges of conscience, and in a rare burst of Scotch generosity, offered his tenants free passage to Canada.

Two shiploads of displaced Scots sailed from Stornoway, and after a rough passage arrived in Quebec. Here the land speculators and their agents, with title to thousands of acres of land advertised "nearly free" in Britain, awaited the horde of settlers. The land, divided into immense tracts, was being actively promoted at dockside. Among them were the Huron Tract, under the persuasive management of "Tiger" Dunlop, of Goderich, and the much more fertile Talbot Settlement, in the Chatam–St. Thomas area being colonized by "Tough Tommy" Talbot.

Some of the Scots elected to stay in Quebec. The rest, 109 families, moved on to Goderich, a town on the east coast of lower Lake Huron. Here, in 1852, they completed their plans, and then all moved to Huron Township, in the County of Bruce, Tiger Dunlop's Huron Tract, to begin their "new life" under pioneering circumstances.

The Lewis Settlement, as it was called, was in the center of Huron Township and was often humorously referred to as the settlement of the "Macs"—the McDonalds, MacLays, Macleods, MacLennans, MacLeans, MacFarlanes, MacKays, Macaulays, MacKenzies, MacGaws, MacInneses and Mac-Ivors. But there were others—the Dobsons, the Granvilles, the Bonthrons, the Logies, the Strongs, the Murrays, the Splans, the Inksters, the Clarks, the Wigginses, the Rosses, the Mathesons and the Craigies, a substantial group of Highlanders plunked down in the wilderness along Lake Huron.

As soon as land was cleared and roads became something other than paths, commercial fishing became the initial industry at Southampton, Port Elgin, Inverhuron, Kincardine, and almost wherever an inlet offered some protection. From here the settlers launched their home-built fleets made from oak or rock elm ribs and pine planking. They were mostly double-enders with fore and aft rigs, in this instance the fore going the taller of the two masts. With gaff and boom, foresails, mainsails and sometimes a jib, they forayed far out on Lake Huron, clear out to Yankee Reef, weathering gales and storms that would have dismantled less-sturdy craft. They comprised a bonny Scotch fleet with even bonnier names. The late Captain John A. Macaulay, in 1958, compiled a list of those he could recall, most with poetic names such as *Scottish Chief, Caledonian, Clansman, Robin Hood, Little John, Lady Dufferin, Maple Leaf, White Wings, Annie Laurie, Forester, Red Hide, Oddfellow, Bold MacIntyre, Bonnie Doon, Scotia, Punch Bowl, Scotch Thistle, Mavis, Marlton, Ivanhoe* and *Golden Gate.* And then there was the *Golden Fleece,* sailed by George Macaulay; Gabriel Granville's *Grand Trunk;* "Gypsie John" MacLeod's *Mary MacLeod;* "Salty" Murdock MacDonald's *Water Lily;* "Big George" Macaulay's *Marquis of Lorne;* "Little Tom" MaGaw's *Mayflower;* "Big Angus" Macaulay's *Green Horn;* Malcolm Murray's *Flying Cloud* and Bill Logie's *Nil Desperandum,* the battle cry of a Highland clan.

One of the problems of life in the "Mac" settlements was the progression of nicknames to differentiate the generations. The original fishermen were all quickly given appropriate nicknames, such as "Hollerin' Joe" Granville, but with so many MacDonalds, Maclods, MacLeans, MacIvors, Mac-

Kays, Macaulays, MacKenzies, Dobsons, Logies, Craigies and Mathesons, and so few favorite Scotch given names such as Malcolm, Angus, Ian, Dan, Neil, Murdoch, Hugh and Alex, identification for subsequent generations depended on retaining the nicknames and given names of predecessors. One of the old-timers was called "Kenny the Belt." His son went through life as "Davy the Buckle." Ian M. Macaulay, now an insurance man in Port Dover, recalls that his grandfather was known as "Big Angus," his father John as "Johnny Big Angus." Now, when Ian goes back to Southampton for a visit, the old folks put him in proper perspective when he tells them that he's Ian "Johnny Big Angus" Macaulay.

"The Lewis Settlemant was, of course, another instance of the Scotch wanting to stay together," says Ian A. Macaulay, the historian of the fishing clans. "In Bruce County, rocky and thin-soiled, they found land very similar to their barren acres on the island of Lewis. So, being stubborn in the true Scottish tradition, they passed by the richest land in Ontario, along Lake Erie and the Niagara Escarpment, to settle there. They would have been better off to have listened to "Tough Tommy" Talbot. But then they would probably have ended up as farmers rather then fishermen. And that would have been unfortunate."

# Bibliography

Alden, Commander John D. *American Steel Navy*. American Heritage Press, 1973.

————. "When Airpower Rode on Paddle Wheels." U.S. Naval Institute *Proceedings*.

Alpena, Michigan. *Argus*. August 23, 1899.

Baxter, James P. III. *The Introduction of the Ironclad Warship*.

*Blue Book of American Shipping*. 1898, 1913.

Brewington, M. V. *Shipcarvers of North America*. Dover Publications, 1972.

Brown, W. M., M.D. "The Queen's Bush."

Chicago, Illinois. *Tribune*. "The Great November Storm." November 17, 1968.

Cleveland, Ohio. *News*. April 27, 1944.

Cleveland, Ohio. *Plain Dealer*. August 31, 1911.

————. July 13, 14, 1915.

————. December 1, 1934.

————. April 29, 1937.

————. November 13, 1940.

————. April 28, 29, 1944.

Detroit, Michigan. *News*. December 1, 1934.

Document No. 98. Senate Document, 26th Congress, Second Session, p. 382.

Document No. 471. House Document, 56th Congress, First Session, pp. 19–28.

Fort William, Ontario. *Times-Journal*. August 31, 1911.

————. August 19, 1969.

*Lloyd's Register of Shipping*
*Lloyd's Register of Yachts*
London, Ontario. *The Western Advertiser*. November 5, 1902.
Ludington, Michigan. *Daily News*. November 12, 13, 14, 1940.
Mansfield, J. B. *History of the Great Lakes*. Chicago: J. H. Beers & Co., 1899.
*Marine Review*. October, 1911.
Muskegon, Michigan. *Chronicle*. December 1, 1934.
———. September 14, 1968.
———. November 12, 13, 14, 1940.
———. May 26, 31, 1972.
Ontario Department of Lands and Forests. *Otter Creek Conservation Report*. 1962.
*Pictorial Marine History*. December, 1940.
Pittsburgh, Pennsylvania. *Press*. "The Old Girl of Erie." July 10, 1955.
Port Huron, Michigan. *Times-Herald*. "Tragedy of the Hunter Savidge." Dorothy Mitts.
———. July 13, 1915.
Port Stanley, Ontario. *News*. June 29, 1972.
Quaife, Milo M. "The Iron Ship." Burton Historical Collection, Detroit Public Library.
Rodebaugh, Donna McLeod. "The Story of Captain Hugh Donald McLeod."
Saginaw, Michigan. *News*. "The Hunter Savidge: Lake Huron's Ghost Ship." August 17, 1969.
Sarnia, Ontario. *Observer*. July 13, 1915.
Sebewaing, Michigan. *Blade-Crescent*. October 12, 1967.
Sheboygan, Michigan. *Press*. October 28, 1972.
Spencer, Herbert Reynolds. "The U.S.S. *Michigan*, U.S.S. *Wolverine*." 1969.
*Time* Magazine. January 25, 1960.
Thunder Bay, Ontario. *News-Chronicle*. June 25; July 7, 10; August 3, 1971.
———. December 1, 2, 1971.
Toledo, Ohio. *Times*. November 8, 1947.
U.S. Lake Survey, Corps of Engineers. *The Great Lakes Pilot*.
U.S. Lifesaving Service. *Annual Report*. 1899.
U.S. Naval Institute. *Proceedings*. No. 260, Vol. 60, pp. 1687–1694.
U.S. Weather Bureau. *The Midwest Storm of November 1940*.
Wolff, Dr. Julius F., Jr. "Shipwrecks of Lake Superior, 1900–1909." *Inland Seas*. Summer, 1971.

# Index